# Food Is Culture

Arts and Traditions of the Table

## Arts and Traditions of the Table
### Perspectives on Culinary History

Albert Sonnenfeld, series editor

Massimo Montanari

# Food Is Culture

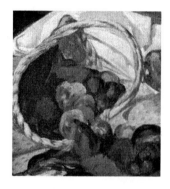

Translated from the Italian by

Albert Sonnenfeld

Columbia University Press

New York

Columbia University Press

*Publishers Since 1893*

New York    Chichester, West Sussex

Copyright © 2004, Gius, Laterza & Figli, Roma-Bari

Translation copyright © 2006 Columbia University Press

Columbia University Press wishes to express its appreciation for assistance given
by the Italian Cultural Institute in the preparation of this translation.


Library of Congress Cataloging-in-Publication Data

Montanari, Massimo, 1949–

    [Cibo come cultura. English]

    Food is culture / Massimo Montanari ; translated from the Italian by Albert
Sonnenfeld.

        p.   cm. — (Arts and traditions of the table)

    Includes bibliograpical references and index.

    ISBN 978-0-231-13790-4 (hard cover : alk. paper)

    1. Food—History.   2. Food habits—History.   I. Title.

TX353.M718513 2006

641.3—dc22

Columbia University Press books are printed on permanent
and durable acid-free paper.

Printed in the United States of America

c 10 9 8 7 6 5 4

# Contents

# Contents

# Series Editor's Preface

As Series Editor of Arts and Traditions of the Table, I have dared for once to assert a *droit du seigneur* to be allowed the pleasure of translating from the Italian this elegantly written essay. I have thoroughly enjoyed that privilege.

At all times reader-friendly and refreshingly unpedantic, *Food Is Culture*, by a world-renowned historian of food and culture, is the kind of book that captivates neophytes and dazzles the experts. We witness here a brilliant synthesizing summation of Massimo Montanari's lifelong reflections on the culinary questions he has analyzed *microscopically* as historiographer and medievalist during his distinguished scholarly career. Here he writes not as a culinary historian *per se* but as an interdisciplinary, always historically grounded anthropologist. By that I mean that his synthesis is unlike the almost platonically abstract structuralist anthropology of Lévi-Strauss in *The Raw and the Cooked*. Montanari proceeds diachronically as a historian must; yet he sees nutrition, literature, linguistics, myth, folklore, history, and medicine in the broadest perspective possible, under a *macroscope,* as it were.

Montanari has organized his materials into short, epigrammatically formulated chapters, subsumed into four interrelated, longer parts: how food came to be; how it came to be cooked; how it came to taste good; how it became metaphor and discourse. On every page there are interdisciplinary insights into countless patterns of culinary behavior and tradition that we have long taken for granted.

Few can resist the inevitable Italian appetizer of *prosciutto-melone*. It takes Montanari's broad cultural perspective to link this refined combination to Galienus's theory of the Four Humors (Dry, Moist, Hot, and Cold), which, in the Hippocratic tradition of antiquity, need to be in healthy balance. So the *dry* prosciutto ham is balanced by the *moist* melon, as lamb is with mint jelly, and game with fruit chutneys. The succulent pear so fashionable in many starter salads today is poised on fresh water-laden greens but finds its dry counterweight in cheese and walnuts.

Why, he asks, are most tables rectangular today, when we have supposedly abandoned the strictly hierarchical power structure of the Middle Ages? However, we still refer to the host as sitting at the "head of the table," and class-based protocol determines to whom will belong the honor of sitting to the right or left of the "head." Oxbridge colleges, even in today's "Cool [Labor Party] Britannia," still have their "high tables."

Whimsically, Montanari alludes to the well-known literary romance legend (of medieval origin) of the Round Table. By making himself merely "first among equals," a topography possible only in a circle, King Arthur attempted to dampen heated hierarchical quarrels among his knights. A new social model might call on an ever-enlarging circumference to make the table genuinely tribal: a theater in the round, so to speak, versus a proscenium-dominated rectangle. *The Last Supper*, for example, pictures Christ at the center of a rectangular table.

The reader may share my own fascination with Montanari's paradigm of a grammar of food. He likens the repertory of animal and plant products to morphemes (the basic units of meaning), comprising a lexicon that is endlessly redefined by environmental, economic, and cultural circumstances. The meal constitutes a syntax, the sequence of modified nouns coordinating main dishes (meat or grain, for example, functioning as central nominative protagonists) with complementary or accompanying dishes preceding, accompanying or following. Sauces, spices or flavorings fulfill further adjectival or adverbial functions. So a meal may be diagrammed or parsed, with various syntactical choices dictated by historical, social, and political factors. In case a verb like "parse" disconcerts, I should remind the reader that none of Montanari's chapters are longer than fifteen pages; nor do his constructs ever descend into theoretical abstruseness!

Throughout *Food Is Culture* there is an underlying proposition that all food is cultural, even "artifact," however artless it may seem. What humans grow involves selectivity, of course, but even in the wildest "natural" or spontaneous growth and "wild" livestock, those elements of biological or horticultural environment and genetics that constitute "natural selection" are "cultural." And from the moment humans choose food products, however "natural" their provenance, that too becomes a cultural choice. With the "discovery" and human appropriation of fire, plants and animals are metamorphosed into cultural manifestations through the crucible of flames and heat: *la cucina* leads to the kitchen, which leads in turn to "cuisine." The richness and resonance of that word *la cucina* here stands revealed. Man forges in the smithy of the fire the created consciousness of his environment, his mythology, his history, his economy, and his gastronomy.

Food as culture? Food *is* culture!

Albert Sonnenfeld

# Introduction

We only too readily associate the idea of food with the idea of nature. That linkage is, however, ambiguous and fundamentally inaccurate. The dominant values of the food system in human experience are, to be precise, not defined in terms of "naturalness," but result from and represent cultural processes dependent upon the taming, transformation, and reinterpretation of Nature.

"A thing not of nature." That is how food had been defined by the doctors and philosophers of antiquity, beginning with Hippocrates, who included it among the factors of life that belong not to the "natural" order but to the "artificial" order of things. Or rather to the *culture* that man himself constructs and manages.

Such a connotation accompanies food all along the pathway that leads it to the mouth of man. Food is culture *when it is produced*, even "performed," because man does not use only what is found in nature (as do all the other animal species) but seeks also to *create* his own food, a food specific unto himself, superimposing the action of production on that of predator or hunter.

Food becomes culture *when it is prepared* because, once the basic products of his diet have been acquired, man transforms them by means of fire and a carefully wrought technology that is expressed in the practices of the kitchen. Food is culture *when it is eaten* because man, while able to eat anything, or precisely for this reason, does not in fact eat everything but rather *chooses* his own food, according to criteria linked either to the economic and nutritional dimensions of the gesture or to the symbolic values with which food itself is invested. Through such pathways food takes shape as a decisive element of human identity and as one of the most effective means of expressing and communicating that identity.

The considerations I propose in these pages are the fruit of research and reflections arising from my specific expertise in the field of medieval history, but developed in a free and open-minded way. I cross chronological and disciplinary boundaries, venturing more as a tourist than as a resident into territories I know only marginally. I quite like on occasion to confront ongoing anthropological and sociological debates, which I do not regard as professional or disciplinary contaminations; rather, I view them as indispensable instruments for understanding themes and ideas that matter to me. Nor do I exclude the very concept of *culture*, which I have used here in a broad, inclusive way. On the contrary, I am certain of having fallen headlong into imprecision and artlessness. I should also perhaps have discussed that concept in more problematic terms.

I have allowed myself a light approach, limiting myself to rethinking in new interpretive frameworks a not inconsiderable number of things I have studied and pondered over the years.

I do not aspire to making a contribution to the theoretical discussion of the meaning of culture and the cultural identities of human experience. I am certain, on the other hand, that numerous suggestions outside my own field contributed to the more effective illumination of important aspects of the story I wanted to tell in this book.

Food Is Culture

# Creating One's Own Food

# Nature and Culture

"... And man created his plants and his animals": thus writes Edward Hyams in his book devoted to the invention of agriculture and the practices of raising and domesticating animals. For the first societies of hunters and gatherers, exploitation of natural resources sufficed. Subsequently, the growth of the population and the need to procure larger quantities of food gradually gave rise to diverse societies devoted to agriculture and to raising livestock; to societies producing their own food, choosing available resources, and intervening in a more active manner in defining environmental equilibrium.

This transition from a hunting economy to an economy of production represented a decisive change both in the relationship of man to land and in human culture. Nevertheless, this did not exclude mixed forms of provisioning lasting thousands of years and dating from the introduction of agricultural practices in the prehistoric Neolithic age. Furthermore, even in the later historical era, the two models continued to constitute two differing ways of understanding the relationship of man and environment. They became the extreme polarities of a dialectic with multiple material and symbolic implications that, in some form, reach us even now.

The viewpoint guiding us today can in reality be misleading: man in an industrial or postindustrial culture is tempted to recognize a fundamental "naturalness" in agricultural activities, which, given our experience, we consider "traditional." For that reason we are led to describe these activities as "primitive" and "archaic." As for the revolution in production induced by the irruption of industry in the modern world, this can in part be justified. Strangely, however, the invention of agriculture was perceived by ancient cultures in exactly the opposite way.

The mental mind-set of the ancients posits agriculture as the moment of breakthrough and innovation, as the decisive leap that forms "civilized" man, separating him from nature—that is, from the world of animals and "savages" (enigmatic characters who turn up frequently in legends and popular folk traditions throughout history and right up to the present day). The fact is that the domestication of plants and the taming of animals in some way gives man the power to make himself the ruler of the natural world, to proclaim himself exempt from the relationship of total dependency in which he had always lived (or rather, in which he *imagined* he had always lived, because even the utilization and exploitation of the land through hunting and gathering entailed a savoir faire, a knowledge, a *culture*). This breakthrough is embodied in exemplary fashion in the mythology of many peoples who had become sedentary farmers. In legends and in folktales, in the myths of the origins of farming, they portray the invention of agriculture as a violent act against Mother Earth, a blow struck by the plow, a world devastated by irrigation projects and works of rural organization: hence the fertility rituals whose purpose was, explicitly or implicitly, to expiate a sin committed against Mother Earth.

The basic aggressiveness of that act seems to confirm, from a historical perspective, the strongly expansive character of agricultural societies, which tend to establish mechanisms for demographic growth unknown to hunters and gatherers—whereas the latter (as demonstrated by ethnographic studies of surviving groups of this type; for example, African pygmies) practice rigorous birth control, aimed at stabilizing the density of the population, which, in the event of uncontrolled growth, could not survive with that kind of economy. Agricultural populations, in contrast, develop, along with domestic settlement, a tendency to growth and to the conquest of new spaces to cultivate. As a consequence, recent studies consider it probable that agriculture on earth did not spread in many places simultaneously but was instead the fruit (as archeological, linguistic, and, finally, genetic data demonstrate) of the expansion of human groups starting from a well-defined territorial nucleus, located on the plateaux of the Near and Middle East—the so-called Fertile Crescent.

There, agriculture was born some 10,000 years ago, gradually conquering the territories of central Eastern Asia (9,000 years ago) and of America (land-linked then to Asia at the current Bering Strait (8,000 years ago). In the opposite direction, Europe was settled and farmed (between 8,000 and 6,000 years ago). As to the reason that all this happened, scholars are in substantial agreement: the invention of agriculture must have been fundamentally a matter of necessity, tied to demographic growth, and to the fact that the economy of hunting and gathering no longer sufficed, perhaps because climatic and environmental changes had made forested zones arid and unproductive. Then, demographic processes began to accelerate of their own momentum.

Selected among the plants for cultivation were the most productive and nutritious, particularly grains, which benefited from special care and attention. Each area of the world had its grain of choice: wheat spread in the Mediterranean regions, sorghum on the African continent, rice in Asia, corn in America.

Around these plants—"the plants of civilization," as the French historian Fernand Braudel felicitously defines them—was organized the entire life of those societies: economic relationships, forms of political power; cultural iconography, and religious rituals (aiming at propitiating the gods to ensure fertility and an abundance of food).

The very creation of the city, perceived by the ancients as the place par excellence for the development of civilization (as is shown by the semantic overlap in Latin between *civitas* and *civilitas*, city and civilization) would be inconceivable without the development of agriculture, either on a material level (the accumulation of goods, riches, technology) or on a mental plane (the idea that man becomes his own master and separates himself from nature by creating his own space in which to live).

In this process of development, human societies have never simply adapted to the conditions imposed by the environment. At times societies have modified them, sometimes in profound ways, introducing cultures from outside the indigenous areas and changing the landscape itself as a result. One need only think of the rice-growing culture of northeast Asia, or the wine-growing culture in north Central Europe—the latter a veritable technological wager against environmental conditions, launched in the Middle Ages and continued into the modern era.

It is in this cultural context that the first agrarian societies, though deeply rooted in the natural rhythms of the cycle of the seasons, evolved the idea of a "civil man" who *artificially* and artfully created food itself—a food not existing in nature, and one that served precisely to mark *the difference between nature and culture*, in order to distinguish the identity of animals from that of man.

In the Mediterranean region—the zone of wheat—it is bread that reveals this symbolic as well as nutritional function: bread does not exist in nature and only man knows how to make it, having elaborated a sophisticated technology which envisages a series of complex operations, the fruit of long experiments and thoughtful reflection (from the cultivation of the grain to the preparation of the finished product). Bread therefore symbolizes man's exit from the animal kingdom and the establishment of "civilization."

In the epic poems *The Iliad* and *The Odyssey,* "bread eaters" are synonymous with "men." Similarly, the epic of *Gilgamesh,* the first literary text known, written in Mesopotamia around 4,000 years ago, tells of a "wild man" who left his status as a minor only at the moment when he learned of the existence of bread, something revealed to him by a *woman*—in fact, a prostitute (granting the female figure in this way both the role of guardian of food knowledge and that of custodian of sexuality). Furthermore, all of this "literary" material seems to correspond to historical reality. Indeed, scholars are pretty well in agreement in acknowledging a *female* priority in the work of observation and selection of the plants that accompanied the birth of agriculture around the first village settlements.

A similar symbolic role was played by wine and beer—fermented beverages that, like bread, do not exist in nature but represent an outgrowth of knowledge and of a complex technology. Man had learned to dominate the natural processes, adapting them for his own benefit.

What we call *culture* takes its place where tradition and innovation intersect. Tradition is made up of knowledge, techniques, values, which were handed down to us. Innovation exists insomuch as this knowledge, these techniques, these values modify the place of man in the environmental context, rendering him able to experience a new reality. *A very successful innovation:* that is how we could define tradition. *Culture* is the interface between these two perspectives.

# Even Nature Is Culture

In the historical development of human societies, a "domestic" economy based on agriculture and livestock raising contrasts with a primitive, undomesticated economy in the acquisition of food: raising animals, or hunting them; cultivating the fruits of the earth, or picking them in their wild state. From this point of view, the opposition between the two food models goes through both animal and vegetable kingdoms. In addition, a second opposition, parallel to the first, is one between stationary settlement and nomadism. From this point of view the perspective changes, because livestock raising and hunting, both of them practiced in uncultivated and wooded spaces, reintegrate the same semantic (and, so to speak, ecological) arena, contrasting broadly with the sedentary, immobile images of the culture of farming. In this sense the dialectic of cultivated fields versus virgin forests, which embodies the opposition of culture and nature, tends to set plants against animals, vegetables against meat products (or in any case animal derivatives such as dairy products).

In farming and sedentary societies the principal ritual and fertility myths that accompany them have as their protagonists the grains and the cycle of seasons. One recalls the story of Persephone. The daughter of Demeter, goddess of the Earth and of agriculture, was abducted by Hades, the god of hell, and restored to her mother on the condition that she return throughout eternity to the underworld for one third of each year. The story is one of an obviously propitiatory character in which is symbolized the sowing of the grain. Underground and dormant during the cold season, the seed will be reborn with the first breath of springtime, thus assuring, with the growth of the vegetation, food for mankind.

Other plants, in other civilizations, play the same role: rice is the protagonist in many Asian legends and narratives, whereas the mythology of the ancient American peoples is largely taken up with corn. According to Mayan legend, the gods built and sculpted man himself out of corn flour, as if to say that without corn there would be no men.

Even in societies of hunters and shepherds, there appear myths and rituals of an identical propitiatory significance, but with animals as protagonists. For example, among the hunting peoples of Europe and Asia there was the tradition of gathering the bones of slain animals (bears, reindeer, stags), taking care that the bones didn't fragment or get lost. The bones were then buried along with the skin, in the belief that by being kept together the soul would return to the bones of the animal, thereby causing it to be reborn.

This myth of the prodigious, fabulous rebirth of animals is also present in Germanic legends, where we meet this "Grande Maiale," or the Great Hog (the imaginary enemy of the Great Earth Mother, or Demeter). At the court of Odin the flesh of the Grande Maiale sufficed to feed all the heroes who had died in battle, since every day "the hog was boiled and cut up to be distributed for meals, yet every evening it was once again made whole." Thus it is told in the *Edda*, the oldest Nordic poem, written in the Middle Ages but expressing an even older, orally transmitted culture.

These examples show us that the opposition between culture and nature is in large part fictitious. "Civilized" man portrayed himself as living outside of nature, but nature herself, in the experience of history, became a conscious cultural model, an intellectual alternative choice to culture. This holds true not only for eras distant from our own, which produced myths and rituals not taken into consideration here, but also in more recent historical periods. In medieval Europe, the dynamic of wild vs. domesticated feeds a continuing debate on means of production and on the lifestyle choices these imply. Especially compelling is the opposition between the traditional Greco-Roman production model, founded on agriculture, and the Germanic one, based on exploitation of the virgin forests (harvesting, hunting, livestock-raising).

But it is precisely during the medieval period that the relationship between the two food models begins to change. Until then these models had been the symbol of two differing civilizations, one of which—the Roman—deprecated the other as inferior and "barbarous." When the "barbarians" invaded the empire and little by little took possession of it, taking over the reins of power, their culture (as well as their food) caught on and became "fashionable," as always happens with the lifestyle of the conquerors—as the "American Way of Life" of the twentieth century has taught us. Hunting and grazing in the woods were no longer viewed as unseemly and "uncultivated" activities; on the contrary, they became the touchstones of a new economy.

At the same time, however, the Roman agricultural tradition spread among the barbarians, whether through the continuing prestige of that tradition or through the mediation of the Christian faith, itself up and coming and "in fashion" in the early centuries of the medieval period. It was not by chance that Christianity, born and nourished in the Mediterranean cultural sphere, had taken up the bread, wine, and oil of the Greco-Latin tradition as its own liturgical symbols. From the intersection of these two trajectories that fused with one another was launched a new food culture, which we recognize today as "European." This culture put on equal footing the eating of bread or meat, and farming or the exploitation of the forest.

From that moment onward the two models of food production were no longer symbolic of two divergent cultural options but, rather, different facets of one and the same system of values. This was a system based on the complicity and the ongoing reciprocity of the agrarian economy and the forest economy, the two models that the Greeks and Latins had contrasted as embodiments, respectively, of culture and nature. Represented here were two expressions of culture, two differing ways of structuring the relationship of man and his environment. From this coupling was born a food regimen characterized principally by the *variety* of the available resources and of the foodstuffs consumed, a variety that gave rise to the extraordinary richness of the European nutritional and gastronomic heritage, which even today is unique in the world.

# Playing with Time (and Climate)

The dynamic between nature and culture examined in the previous chapter also finds expression in the complexity of the relationships (often ambiguous) established by traditional societies to the idea of time. By this I mean the seasonality of farm produce and agricultural products, the annual growth rhythms of plants and animals, as well as the relationship of food to climate itself.

Optimal harmonization of one's own rhythms of life with those of nature has always been a basic human requirement. Nevertheless, to do so means simultaneously pursuing the goal of controlling, modifying, and in some way countermanding "natural" weather. Despite the romanticism of certain poetic images describing a balance, or a perfect symbiosis between man and nature in traditional societies, various conceptualizations of a utopia, and plans to bring it about, were always for a world in which the seasons did not exist and time was perfectly controllable because it was not subject to evolution and changes.

Eden, the earthly paradise in the biblical narrative, did not know seasons. There, an eternal springtime offered mankind perennially fresh food, always available, always consistent. The same was true in the Land of Cockaigne, that magical place of perpetual plenty dreamed up by the popular imagination of the medieval and early modern eras. Science and technology (at first in the world of agricultural economies, then driven by the industrial revolution) have always been at the service of this project, following two lines of action: *prolonging* time, and *stopping* it. The strategies for attaining this goal have been, respectively, diversification of the species and acquiring the techniques of preserving foodstuffs.

The first goal was to differentiate species in order to make them produce as much as possible over the long haul in the course of the year. Agronomic texts of every era have given extraordinary attention to this goal. The multiplication of the number of cultivated species, the attention paid to the diversification of their time of flowering and growth aimed at overcoming, as much as possible, the natural limits of production. A typical example was the selection and cultivation of the greatest number of varieties of apples, pears, and other fruit. Time and weather *were extended* to make foods available during a stretch of months at times almost unimaginable compared to today's practices.

During certain periods of history, the propagation of multiple varieties was a skill honored by horticultural specialists. The famous experiments of "the director of all royal gardens" (those of King Louis XIV), Jean de la Quintinye, are detailed in his *Practical Guide for Fruit and Vegetable Gardens* (first edition 1690), a text which still remains the masterpiece of premodern "pomology," or fruit cultivation. De la Quintinye concentrated particularly on pears, projecting an orchard of five hundred varieties that at any time of the year would be able to provide fresh fruit for the sovereign's table. On the other hand, this kind of special care was not totally new: *The Treatise on Trees* by Giovanni Soderini, in the second half of the sixteenth century, reviewed a great variety of cultivated species, specifying what for each of these would be the optimum period for consumption and the best nutritional use thereof.

The peasants, too, in their own way, had always followed this path: trees of differing species, in the cultivated garden and in the field, sufficed to dislocate in time the growth pattern of the fruits. More generally, the peasants sought, within the limits of what was possible, to vary the resources available to them. I am thinking of the multiplicity of grains cultivated during the high Middle Ages to compensate for the poor crop yield each grain had offered. To cultivate rye, oats, millet or, spelt, as well as wheat and barley, was a way of fighting the vicissitudes of climate. Varying both the times for growing plants and the times for harvesting provided security measures for protection against possible climatic disasters that technology was all but powerless to remedy. In the agricultural societies that still exist in the world, the diversification of resources is the primary instrument for guaranteeing adequate food supplies for the local population (whereas monocultures, utilized by agroindustrial operations, are the fruits of an economic and political colonization that serves other interests).

The second objective was to develop efficient methods for conserving vegetable and animal products for use beyond their *natural* cycle of growth. The food of country people, in particular, has always focused on produce and foodstuffs that are preservable in the long term. This initially meant concentrating above all on such foods as cereals and vegetables, which could be preserved for many months, even years, simply by storing them in dry places, above or below ground.

As for perishable foods, in the course of many centuries much energy has been devoted to developing a great variety of techniques for preserving them over time. "Canning is anxiety in its absolute state," wrote the sociologist Giralmo Sineri. But it is also a bet on the future: "Who would ever make marmalades if he didn't have the hope of living at least long enough to be able to eat them?"

In ancient times one tried to keep foods as nature produced them by insulating them from the air. For example, Aristotle advised burying the apple in a layer of clay. But the most frequently used method of preservation was drying, carried out in the heat of the sun (where the climate permitted it) or else with smoke (in colder climes). But more usually, and everywhere, one had recourse to salt, the hero of the very first stratum of food history itself, because, in addition to flavoring foods, salt had the chemical property of drying them and therefore preserving them over time. Meats, fish, and greens have always been preserved with salt, and this itself constituted the principal guarantee of sustenance in a rural economy that could not entrust itself to the daily market or the capriciousness of the seasons. So we can quite properly and correctly think of the taste of salt as characteristic, throughout history, of the cuisine of the poor.

Other processes for preserving goods were vinegar and oil based (the former more readily available than the second), or involved the use of honey and sugar. The latter, introduced into Europe during the Middle Ages, long remained a privilege of the happy few, and only at the beginning of the nineteenth century did it cast off its elitist character. Then for several centuries an opposition between sweet and salty tastes emerged as attributes of socially and economically differentiated food models. In general, however, all these substances (salt as well as sugar, honey as well as vinegar and oil) made products "preservable" only at the price of modifying their original taste to a greater or lesser degree.

This very same principle, manipulating or modifying the natural quality of foodstuffs, was applied to a technique as widespread as that of fermentation itself. Decisive from a cultural (or symbolic) point of view as an expression of the human capacity for turning a natural process in itself negative to its own positive advantage by controlling it, man made putrefaction a means to a useful end. From this negative capacity were born extraordinary inventions such as cheese and other milk derivatives, prosciutto ham, and other cured meats that combine fermentation with salting. The acidic fermentation of greens such as cabbage was used in north central areas of Europe (*sauerkraut*), as well as in China, Japan, and other parts of the world.

Only the use of cold (in addition to the hermetic "sealing" Aristotle writes about) could allow forms of preserving more respectful of the natural origins of the products. Ever since ancient times, snow and ice were harvested and used for this purpose, both in privately held buildings (the ice shed of the manor house or farms) as well as public facilities (in Paris, the last ice warehouse was built in the middle of the nineteenth century). The cold storage or refrigeration industry, which also came to the fore during the nineteenth century, made available the first refrigerators and, later, deep-freeze technology signaled a decisive turn toward the possibility of preserving foods without modifying their original taste.

The methods of preserving foods, developed and driven in response to famine and hunger, quickly exceeded such parameters through a kind of technological transfer that has applied them to high gastronomy. Thus were born many refined products destined for the marketplace. One thinks of charcuterie and of cheeses, or of the great tradition of marmalades, "typical products" these, that constitute an essential part of our gastronomic heritage. In such ways are revealed essential, hitherto unsuspected, ties between the world of hunger and the world of pleasure.

Invention is not born only from luxury and power but also from necessity and from poverty. The fascination of culinary history is basically this: to discover how mankind, with effort and imagination, has sought to transform the pangs of hunger and the anguish of nutritional privation into potential occasions for pleasure.

# Playing with Space

The struggle for mastery of space is a kind of alternative (or variant) to the game of playing with time: getting food from other more or less distant places, overcoming the restrictive limitations of region or locale, and transcending food's seasonal variability. This quest for mastery of space is an ancient practice that remained a social privilege for thousands of years, better still a *sign* of social privilege. As Cassiodorus, minister to King Theodorus, wrote in the sixth century: "Only the ordinary citizen is satisfied with what local surroundings can provide. The prince's table must offer such a variety of food as to cause one to marvel just at the sight." In this way the prince configures and celebrates his diversity.

Actions aiming to overcome spatial and temporal limitations intersect and reinforce each other. But with the passage of centuries, the former tends to become progressively more important than the latter. The phenomenon is already apparent in the medieval period with the expansion of commercial trade. It becomes ever more evident with the increasingly frequent voyages around the world, beginning in the sixteenth century. The decisive step forward comes during the nineteenth and twentieth centuries thanks to the revolution in transportation, linked to industrialization. Transportation allowed the problems of food supply to be resolved elsewhere, thereby diminishing the previously determining factors of produce diversification and preservation, or at least joining these to other, more significant burdens.

The relationship of men to space, after all, has now radically changed, having expanded until it exploded into the logic of the "global village." Today, in the industrialized countries, one can find *fresh* produce at any time of the year, using the total world system as one production and distribution zone. This constitutes a true revolution, if we refer to the new planetary dimension of the food economy and to the breadth of the social structures involved. At least in the wealthy countries, the mechanisms of the global market and the dramatic lowering of prices have expanded, at least potentially, the consumer sector to the near totality of the population. On a cultural level, however, this revolution is only apparent: the needs and desires that the revolution satisfied were old needs and desires, though once fulfilled within more limited spaces and for fewer consumers.

Head Chef at the Mantua court of the Gonzagas in the seventeenth century and author of an important culinary treatise, Bartolomeo Stefani offers some acute reflections on the themes of space and time. His treatise observes that foods are actually never "out of season." "Do not be astonished," he wrote, "if in these writings of mine, on certain occasions I order some things, as for example foods such as asparagus, artichokes, peas and the like in the months of January or February, when at first glance they would seem out of season." Do not be astonished if on 27 November 1655, at the banquet staged in honor of Queen Christina of Sweden, visiting Mantua during her trip to Rome, "I ordered as first course (and on the 27th of November!) strawberries in white wine." Italy (today we would say the earth herself)—Stefani asserted—is so rich in good things that it would be a sin not to put them on the table of gourmets. Faced with such abundance and generosity—here Stefani inserts a list of regional specialties—why shut oneself within one's own narrow horizon? Why limit oneself "to the bread from one's own native hearth?" In reality "a good horse and a full purse" suffice (stated otherwise: rapid means of transportation and sufficient funds) to find elsewhere, fresh and in all seasons, "all those good things I propose here!"

*A good steed and a well-filled purse.* Freighters and international trucks (*TIR*) fill our supermarkets, lowering, along with prices, the images of prestige that have always accompanied exotic products. Today the distinction of the up-market has shifted elsewhere: paradoxically, back to the long reviled "terroir." But we shall return to this later.

# Conflicts

". . . And Man created his plants and his animals." But this "man" historically does not exist. He is an abstraction embodied in real people, who live in more or less complex societies, inside of which power struggles and conflicts for control of resources are an ongoing reality. In this light we ought to reconsider many things already stated here, observing that conflicts, broadly speaking, take on varying characteristics according to whether they develop within individual communities that are socially and culturally cohesive; or whether they involve various relationships among very diverse communities and cultures.

In simpler societies the kind of opposition that exists is between the ruling and lower classes within individual communities or territories. For example, the feudal society of the European Middle Ages witnessed the emergence of a dominant group of "lords" who controlled farmwork, forest exploitation, and commercial exchanges. In a word, they controlled the nexus of the economy and production of food. In this context the peasant rebellions or, more commonly, the protests (which rarely assumed the weight and breadth of true rebellions) had as their target the retention of already acquired rights and privileges. Such protests happened, in particular, when lordly prerogatives tended to exclude collective use of forest privileges by reserving hunting and grazing rights for the nobility. As Rodney Hilton observed, the popularity of such legends as that of Robin Hood reflected not only the fascination of adventure stories for the marginals of society, but also "utopian images of a world in one could freely hunt and eat meat." Freedom of access to natural resources was a pivotal motive in the demands of the English peasants in 1381, as it was in those of the German peasants in 1525.

In Italy, a land of stronger urban traditions, similar forms of control and domination were practiced by the cities on the surrounding lands, which during the Middle Ages took on the name of "countryside" (*contado*, from which comes "contadino" or peasant). This is defined as an area with control by the city over all phases of food production: the work of the farmers, the distribution of produce through markets, and forms of artisanal food craftsmanship in both countryside and cities. And, in this case as well, a dominant ruling group (the social class in power in the cities) succeeded in imposing an alimentary "order," which had as its prime goal satisfying its own needs (along with providing produce for the city markets and consumers). This hierarchical order turned out not infrequently to be to the detriment of the subject class of consumers in the rural community.

Tensions exploded above all in times of food shortage or famine, when the inhabitants of the countryside crowded at the gates of the city in search of food and, in the most dramatic cases, were violently driven away from the portals.

More complex are the transverse (lateral) conflicts that take place not within a single social and political entity but between one society (its dominant group) and another.

Referring once again to the preceding examples, if a feudal lord or a city controls the resources of a subject territory, then at the same time tensions and conflicts can arise with other lords and cities. These can result in a relationship of "dominant /dominated," that is, "master/servant," between the two parallel institutions. Among the lords possessing castles, there came about, between the tenth and twelfth centuries, a process of selection that led to the construction of specific hierarchies, both political and economic, among the various powers.

The same thing happened among the cities: the larger conurbations placed the smaller ones under their control. For example, in the second half of the thirteenth century, Bologna taxed centers under its control with the payment of a certain quantity of grain, and other foods to be consigned, even when sufficient quantities were unavailable because of inadequate harvests. In this last case the subject communities were obliged to turn elsewhere to acquire products at external markets, on occasion using money borrowed from the same ruling entity. For example, Bologna lent money to the city of Imola to allow it to purchase products in Romagna or in the Marches, thus instituting as well a form of financial control over the subject city.

At the time of the development of national states, or in any case of more complex political systems, the dominant/dominated relationship also applied on a larger scale. Typical was the case of modern England, which through its class of landowners exercised harsh, restrictive control over the Irish food supply, channeling to England the valuable produce (meats, wheat, etc.), while leaving in place products of lesser commercial or nutritional value. Thanks to this process, the Irish peasants were more or less reduced to eating only potatoes during the nineteenth century, and the double shortfall of 1846–47 decimated the people, forcing many of them to emigrate overseas—and this, not because foodstuffs were totally lacking, but because the economic food distribution system was governed by an inflexible mechanism of mastery of the stronger over the weaker.

On the other hand, beginning with the sixteenth century the control mechanisms of "food space" had enlarged to a worldwide scale, with the establishment of European dominion (state-run and private companies bent on exploiting resources) over the Asian continent and later with Christopher Columbus's "discovery" of America. On all latitudes, the economic balances and the productive structures of "the new continent" were distorted to facilitate exploitation by the European masters, who used the conquered territories as food-producing spaces. From these were exported overseas all the basic components of the European diet—plants and livestock. The ancient Mediterranean plants (the classical triad of grain, vine, and olive) as well as the principal grazing animals (cows, horses, pigs) moved during these years beyond the great sea of Oceanus. The same thing happened with coffee and sugarcane, products of Middle Eastern African origins, which the Arabs and Turks had made available to the West and which the Westerners did not hesitate to transplant to the American colonies, in order then to satisfy the new desires of the old continent. This was to initiate an important chapter in the history of colonization and slavery. Less extreme was the transformation of the Asian economies, which nonetheless, like that of the New World, was also largely conditioned by the interests of the European commercial companies and consumers.

The clash between rich and poor countries, despite the good will of the few and the dubious paternalism of the many, reveals ever more clearly the enormous conflict of antithetical interests characterizing today's society. That tension is virtually a broader version—the product of the global economy—of the struggles for the control and exploitation of food resources, which from time immemorial have accompanied human history. Albeit in an extremely modified context, this resurrects the theme of class struggle within what Marshall McLuhan termed "the global village."

# The Invention of Cuisine

# Fire > Cooking > Kitchen > Cuisine > Civilization

What distinguishes the food of men from that of the other animals? Cooking is the human activity par excellence; it is the act of transforming a product "from nature" into something profoundly different.

Man, as we have shown in the preceding pages, in addition to consuming already available resources in nature, learned to produce resources himself by developing the practice of growing plants and raising livestock. Production, however, applies only to the preliminary phase of retrieving food, not to the ways of consuming it. Moreover, man, being omnivorous, chooses food out of individual and collective preferences tied to perpetually changing values, tastes, and meanings. But this subject (which we shall treat more extensively later) does not suffice to identify the ways in which the human race eats, nor why other animal species, albeit in more primitive fashion, develop special habits and differentiated tastes.

Perhaps the principal element of diversity lies in the fact that man, and only man, is capable of lighting and utilizing fire. This technology, along with other procedures, allows him to cook, and to create a kitchen and a cuisine. *Cooking is the human activity par excellence: it is the act that transforms a product "from nature" into something profoundly different.* The chemical modifications induced by cooking, and the combination of ingredients, work together to bring to the mouth a food, that, if not completely "artificial," is surely "created." That is why in ancient myths and in the basic *Ur*-folk tales and legends, the conquest of fire represents (symbolically but also materially and technically) the constitutive and foundational moment of human civilization. The cooked and the raw, to which Claude Lévi-Strauss devoted a justly famous essay, represent the opposite poles of the dialectic (however complex and by no means simple, as we have seen) between nature and culture.

In Greek mythology fire belonged only to the gods, until the day when the Titan Prometheus revealed its secret to men. It was an act of compassion toward these naked and helpless beings that his brother Epimetheus, charged with distributing different talents among living beings, had overlooked in a moment of distraction. To compensate for this forgetfulness Prometheus stole the fire in the workshop of the god Hephaestus and gave it as a gift to men. In this way he became the true artificer or creator of human civilization, which, with this new tool, succeeded in rising above the animal level and learning the techniques of mastering nature. Controlling fire made man a divinity of sorts: no longer a slave, but now the master of natural processes which he had learned to control and to modify. For this deed Prometheus incurred the wrath of the gods and was punished in an exemplary fashion.

The clearest symbolic change of this major happening, made famous and represented by the myth, is reflected in the imagery of the kitchen, which, linked to the use of fire, became a fundamental constituent of human identity. From that moment onwards it was no longer possible to call oneself "man" without cooking one's own food. The rejection of cooking took on (as we shall see) the meaning of a veritable challenge to civilization, equivalent to the rejection of domesticated farming in the practices of food production.

The idea of an artifice that transforms nature governed the activities of the cook for centuries. Forms, colors, textures were modified, shaped, and "created" with techniques expressive of a deliberate distancing from "naturalness." The "typical" cook of premodern cultures, at least until the seventeenth century, was an "artist" in no way respectful of the original qualities of products. The idea of a "natural" cuisine, when and where it subsequently established itself, undercut this image and put forth a new idea of nature (positive rather than negative). This happened many times throughout history—above all, today.

We need, however, to establish that fire and cuisine do not always coincide. On the one hand, to define the culinary act simply as the transformation of foods by means of fire seems reductive. We would thereby effectively see excluded from the realm of cuisine all the preparations not requiring cooking—for example, the refined techniques used by Japanese cooks in the preparation of raw fish. No one would dare to assert that this practice is apart from haute cuisine, even though it does not involve the use of fire.

On the other hand, there are those who believe that cooking foodstuffs is not by itself synonymous with cuisine. As Françoise Sabban has emphasized, in the Chinese tradition, "cooking" and "creating cuisine" are quite different notions. The first simply implies the ability to use fire (hardly sufficient in our perspective to define a realm of "civilization"), whereas the second suggests a technical ability with rich aesthetic and artistic implications.

The Chinese writer Lin Yutang alluded to this distinction in a 1936 essay. He juxtaposed the heights of Chinese cuisine against the impoverishment of "Western cuisine" (actually he is referring to the Anglo-Saxon culinary tradition), which knew only one word, *cooking,* to designate both the act of cooking and the creation of cuisine. In Lin's eyes this betrays a banal approach to food, one aimed only at making foodstuffs edible.

This distinction brings a further element of uncertainty into our discussion. This is not to detract from the ongoing fact that in the symbolic representation that man has historically given of himself, mastery of fire and the cooking of foodstuffs have continued to be perceived as a main element in the formation of human identity and of man's evolution from a wild to a civilized state. Nonetheless, Lin Yutang's distinction makes us think about the multiplicity of meanings of the Italian word *cucina*. *Cucina* (cooking, kitchen, cuisine), in fact, designates a whole range of possibilities, from the simplest to the most complex, from the daily practices of housewives to the virtuoso displays of great specialty chefs.

In general, *cucina* can be defined as an ensemble of techniques for the preparation of foodstuffs. But even in such a broad and simplified meaning of the word one finds that, according to particular societies, times, and places, the ensemble of these techniques can be more or less inclusive. That is, they can include a great variety of procedures, depending on their degree of specialization, their greater or lesser levels of professionalism, and their possible integration into the commercial economy. For example, in a business such as the slaughtering of animals and the butchering of meat, grinding and pounding are excluded from the daily culinary practices in contemporary European societies, although for a time they were a part of those practices. Moreover, grinding and pounding are still part of the culinary practices in numerous traditional rural societies.

In any case, the complexity of kitchen procedures is not linked (as we might erroneously have thought) to the professional level of the cooks. On the contrary, it is precisely in order to prepare the more common subsistence foods that more complex manual techniques, requiring more time and more skill, were perfected. One need only recall the lengthy procedures required for preparing the tortilla in Mexico or couscous in North Africa, or indeed for mortar-and–pestle ground millet in Central Africa, or for making cassava tubers edible in Oceania. Processes like these require hour after hour of highly specialized labor carried out daily by women (the eternal heroines of the kitchen and custodians of the techniques that define cooking), all this handed down by practice and imitation; all this, in traditional societies, is organically included in the idea of cuisine.

In industrialized countries, however, the ensemble of techniques needed for the preparation of daily meals is much more limited and less burdensome, given that a large number of the preliminary tasks have devolved onto professionals, and to the agro-food industry. Moreover, in the industrialized countries, culinary activity tends to forsake the domestic domain to become a profession practiced in the public arena of restaurants. In this new dimension, cooking tends to change genders, becoming no longer a female domestic activity but to a profession exercised principally by men.

# Written Cuisine and Oral Cooking

The contrasts among differing types of society and cuisine, whose essential lines we have barely sketched here, has been a topic for consideration by various scholars, one of whom is the English sociologist Jack Goody.

According to these scholars, only rigorously complex, hierarchical, and centralized societies (of the type that historically had developed in Europe and in Asia) were in a position to produce a professional cuisine that was clearly distinct from a domestic one. In contrast, most tribal or weakly centralized societies in Africa, have only known cooking prepared by women within a familial context.

The culinary treatise (a subcategory of technical literature), which allowed for the collection of kitchen recipes, could have been developed, Goody adds, only in countries with a long written tradition. And with the development of a written record of cuisine which made the cumulative increase of knowledge possible, man has answered the need for an authentic and unique body of information, of a kind unavailable, at least in material tangible form, to societies still clinging to oral traditions. Written cuisine permits the codification, in an established and recognized medium, of the practices and techniques developed by a specific society. Theoretically speaking, orally transmitted cooking, is destined not to leave traces of itself over time.

This destiny would seem to oppose not only the societies with written traditions to those with oral traditions, but also various social groupings within the same societies. It is clear, in fact, that societies within a written tradition like the European had long handed down only, or above all, texts produced by and for the social elites—the aristocrats of the court and the upper urban classes. Because the lower classes did not commit their own experiences to writing but relied on oral transmission, they have seemingly left us nothing. For example, what can we know of the peasant food culture of the Middle Ages?

It is no simple matter to recognize the specific role of peasant society in the structures of food production, in the channels of distribution, and in the symbolic values attributed to behavior and consumption; but a picture does emerge from documentation. More difficult is gaining access to the actual sphere of the kitchen itself, its ways of preparing dishes, and the tastes of its food (which we cannot consider to be solely the domain of the upper classes).

If we take for granted that written culture had been produced by and for the ruling classes, it follows that only the cuisine of the powerful has remained available to us, albeit in a fragmentary form, handed down from documentary and literary sources. Evidently, the oral source was inaccessible to the historian, who wasn't interested in contemporaneity. So we may be forced to remain silent on the cuisine of the poor and illiterate, or at the very most to formulate hypotheses interpolating scattered fragments of historical reality.

A more educated reading of the sources might suggest various paths to follow. Even if written texts are never the *direct* expression of a popular culture, these texts can typify that culture with a greater accuracy than we might have expected. In medieval recipe books, as well as in those of the Renaissance that are an extension of the former, one can perceive a network of continuity between the cuisine of the elites—one that is *explicitly* portrayed—and a different kind of cuisine that can be traced back through popular culture.

The fact remains that the aristocratic and bourgeois culture, while erecting insurmountable behavioral (and primarily culinary) barriers between the ruling and ruled classes, did not exclude a daily convergence of tastes, habits, and traditions. The rigidity of the symbolic patterns or grids opposing the lifestyle of the peasantry to that of its lords and masters (or that of the city-dwellers, according to a typically Italian variation) coexists peacefully with the presence of country produce and peasant flavors in the cuisine of the elite classes. In fact, to some extent it presupposes it. The real contamination between the two cultures somehow renders indispensable the erection of ideological barriers, and of symbols of differentiation and separation. Faced with foods that in the collective mind-set (or at least that of the ruling classes) benefited from a "typically peasant" image, the elites resorted to some simple stratagems to modify such an image and make it compatible with their zone of privilege. Of these strategies, which turn out to offer a special peephole allowing the reconstitution of oral and popular culture, recipe books afford impressive and misunderstood testimony.

The oldest Italian recipe collection, the *Liber de Coquina*—"Book of Cookery" (thirteenth to fourteenth century), from the South—begins with vegetables and does so quite deliberately: "Wishing here to consider cuisine and various foods, we shall initially begin with the easiest things, and that is the category of vegetables." There follow ten different recipes for cabbage, before moving on to spinach, to fennel, and to baby greens, and then on to the treatment of other vegetables: chickpeas, green peas, fava beans, lentils, and beans. But *nota bene*: in literary representations, and in the food *ideology* of the Middle Ages, all these foods belong to the peasant world. Yet the cuisine of the *Liber* is one specifically intended for the ruling classes. The gap between discourse and practice, between word and action, between mental codes and real customs, is obvious. This contrast is powerful and requires equally powerful signals to leave ambiguity behind, and to return to politically correct imagery.

The first sign is that of various combinations and modalities of usage, which immediately clarify the societal destination of the food. The product of humble origins becomes ennobled, so that it can share a different gastronomic and symbolic system, no longer an isolated main course, but now as a simple ingredient (among others) of an upscale variety of foods. As Bologna scholar Sabadino degli Arienti wrote in the fifteenth century, garlic is "always rustic food, but at times becomes artfully civilized when thrust into the body of a roasted duck." From the moment in which garlic is stuffed into a roast goose, its peasant nature is "artificially" modified. Thus, garlic sauce, based on garlic ground in a mortar and typical of country cooking, can also figure in the recipe collections of the upper classes. It all depends on what accompanies it. A fourteenth-century Venetian book proposes it as suitable for "all meats." Similarly, the recipe for "delicate cabbages intended for noble consumption" contained in the *Liber de Coquina* specifies the intended use of the humble vegetable as a side dish or accompaniment to meat dishes: *for all meats.*

The second sign of ennoblement beyond the game of combinations is the *enrichment* of poor produce by the addition of expensive ingredients, especially spices. Consider this recipe from a fourteenth-century Tuscan book: "Take turnips well boiled in water, and put them to sauté in oil, onion and salt. When they are cooked and prepared put spices in the pan." The logic of the discourse is clear: once spiced, any food whatsoever becomes worthy of the master's table. But this implies a common base of gastronomic culture, a societal intersecting of food practices and customs. We can find the same line of tendencies in fifteenth- to sixteenth-century recipe collections, which return to and expand the wholly lower-class popular tradition of greens in the kitchen: cabbage, turnips, fennel, mushrooms, pumpkin, lettuce, parsley, and all sorts of herbs, as well as such vegetables as beans and peas, which are the basis of so many dishes (soups, pastries, crepes) offered by the cookbook of Maestro Martino, the most prestigious Italian cook of the fifteenth century.

If the centrality of vegetables is one of the dominant characteristics of the people's cuisine (and for this reason it is important to verify their importance in the recipe collections of the court), poor people's foods par excellence are polentas and soups made of the cheaper grains, greens, and chestnuts—all key elements of a cuisine distinguished above all by the need to fill one's belly to ward off the specter of hunger, and to ensure daily survival. Be that as it may, this cuisine of the poor also left important traces in the cookbooks used by the upper classes. The crushed fava beans proposed in the early days of the fourteenth century by the *Liber de Coquina* are nothing but a bean polenta, similar to the one which, sometimes known by the name *macco*, is revealed to us in ample documentation as typical peasant food.

Just as significant is the millet with milk proposed by the Tuscan cookbook: "wash and grind the 'vegetable' (so defined by the text, associating millet with the greens), boil and blend it with milk and bacon fat." This is a peasant recipe indeed, were it not for the fact that instead of being the main course of the meal, as was the case for the peasantry, this "paniccia" is served as a side dish to something richer and more substantial: "You can eat this dish with roast kid!"

The cookbooks also suggest polentas based on oatmeal, orzo, and millet, sometimes presented as dishes "for the indisposed," that is, simple, economical, without added spices, but for that reason close to the prototype of the lower-class diet. Spelt, millet, and vegetables show up in the recipes of Maestro Martino, and we can find numerous soups using cheaper grains, chestnuts, and greens in the pages of Bartolomeo Scappi, the most important cook of Renaissance Italy and author of a monumental culinary treatise published in 1570. As we have already seen in the previously discussed example, these polentas and soups are enriched with spices, sugar, and choice meats, but nonetheless can be traced back to a cuisine bearing the marks of its peasant origins. In the works of Scappi there is even mention of a "thick grain," that is, made with corn, a new product with American origins, which the peasantry for a long time had trouble accepting on their own tables.

In Scappi's pages, reference to popular culture in some cases is explicit. Different preparations of fish are derived, the author admits, from the simple recipes of fishermen, to which he would be hard put to add anything. After giving the recipe for turbot "in potaggio," he reveals its origins: "When I was in Venice and in Ravenna, I had learned from fishermen from Chioggia, and from Venetians, who make the best *potaggi*, that along the sea coasts, no one cooked them differently from the way I have stated above." Of course, Scappi adds, "I believe that they succeed better than other cooks because they cook them at the very moment the fish were caught."

All this has an important methodological consequence: It is not true that the culture of the lower classes and the oral tradition that expresses it are irremediably lost. Both were transmitted by written texts and by the dominant ruling-class culture, with substantial and formal documentation also based on the way the preparation of dishes was described and, presumably carried out. In other words, the visibility of peasant cuisine (and thus of popular culture itself) in the cookbooks of the medieval and Renaissance elites (the decisive periods for the formation of Italian gastronomic culture) was enhanced by the specific modalities of the cook's work.

The prevalent procedure is one of accumulation or compounding—one that *adds* noble ingredients to a humble product, or brings together noble products and simple preparations. This means that the starting point is by definition more broadly shared; that the elements of separation or divergence supervened *later*.

This is also worth noting because it constitutes an element of diversity with respect to modern culinary practices. For centuries, in fact, refined cooking—that of the great families and later that of the great restaurants—was characterized not only by the advanced and final phases of culinary method but also, often, by its preliminary phases. The French lesson of the seventeenth and eighteenth centuries, which initiated much of modern culinary method, was also innovative for the introduction of "preps" (court-bouillon, brunoise, roux, etc.) that altered the character of dishes *from the outset*. For this reason the cookbook of a fashionable chef today is hardly comparable to popular cuisine. In whatever mode he expresses or evokes poor people's cuisine, he does so in an indirect way, making for difficult textual decrypting.

If instead the point of departure reflects a commonly shared culinary code or vocabulary—as would seem to be the case in medieval and Renaissance cooking—the reliability of the cookbooks of the elite as mirrors of "peasant" cuisine and as a source for its reconstitution becomes decidedly more pronounced.

The civilization based on written texts can thus allow us to salvage something from an oral culture that, while not recorded directly in writing, has been reflected in an indirect but no less visible way.

# Anticuisine

Cuisine is the very symbol of civilization and of culture; the rejection of cuisine represents a challenge to these values and has the same meaning as the rejection of domesticated agriculture in the practice of food production. The raw, like the wild, takes on symbolic value for "noncultural" choices, which, nonetheless, reveal themselves once again as strongly impregnated with culture.

A typical example is that of hermits who, fully conscious of intellectual coherence, assumed and at times flaunted a pattern of eating that signified self-imposed withdrawal from the world. To that end they first of all denied themselves the use of fire and culinary processes, seen as the bases of "civilized" identity. But in so doing they merely put forth a different kind of culture, a utopian one that looks *beyond* this world.

In Christian tradition, the wild, or uncooked, is an image of food from the myth of Providence, of a happy time when man had not yet sinned or been condemned to earn his bread by the sweat of his brow. The raw has a similar significance in that it is a function of a life plan aiming to forsake sin-ridden humanity in order to regain a prelapsarian divine dimension. Or, paradoxically, the raw seeks to draw nearer to the animal condition that in its nonhuman and noncultural choices is the total opposite of divinity. This is the meaning of certain behavioral patterns found in the first centuries of the Christian experience among the hermits of the Syrian and Egyptian deserts—characters such as Hilarion, of whom it was said that "he fed himself only on wild grasses and the shoots of raw roots."

Numerous analogous examples can be found in the *Storia Lausiaca* and the *Lives of the Fathers*, two fourth-century texts that bring together the life stories of hermits.

Macario Alessandrino "for seven years ate nothing that had been put through fire"; Filoromo "for 18 years abstained from all cooked foods." Sisai, when a youth came to ask him how to behave if he were to attain sainthood, pronounced a judgment as follows: "It is unnecessary for you to cook anything." In the same vein, "do not savor anything cooked" was one of the main ordeals that Dioscoro di Namisia imposed upon himself to test his moral steadfastness and resolution.

This ideological model or archetypal pattern appeared in the West sometime later, albeit with an abrupt change of scenario: replacing the desert, the forest now became the main setting, the place for solitude where one could demonstrate one's asceticism. In the forests of central France, Winnoco practiced ascetic solitude, limiting his food exclusively to "raw wild grasses." In the woods of the Italian Apennines, the hermit Venerio, a disciple of Romualdo, "lived for four years on fruit, grasses and roots, and tasted nothing cooked."

That we are dealing here with strongly intellectual and *cultural* choices is shown by the well-defined awareness of the main characters and of the texts that transmit their deeds. This supposed "nonculture" is acquired according to conventional mechanisms of cultural transmission (the case of Sisai, who passed his teaching on to his disciple, is from this point of view a perfect example). The ideal, however, would be to acquire this nonculture not by having recourse to other men, but by receiving it directly from God or from animals (though of course it is better to be guided by God himself!).

The strange pairing of opposites coinciding in the shared opposition to the human dimension appears in a passage of the *Lives of the*

*Fathers.* There we are told of an ascetic who, withdrawing to the desert to live in perfect solitude, chose to eat nothing but manifestly raw grasses and roots. But the recluse had a problem: he didn't know how to distinguish the good herbs from the bad. He tried them all, but some hid a poisonous core behind a pleasing and inviting appearance. Soon the hermit was seized by indescribable stomach pains, spasms of vomiting, and fevers. Then, afraid that he might die, he became suspicious of everything that seemed edible. He simply stopped eating, again risking death, only this time from starvation. After seven days there came the miracle: a wild goat appeared before him, bringing a bundle of grass the hermit had picked but dared not touch. The goat began to separate the good from the poisonous plants with his mouth, showing the hermit which ones he should eat. From that day on, the holy man, having mastered the precious lesson, succeeded in surviving in the desert by avoiding both hunger and poisoning. This episode is particularly suggestive in expressing the profoundly cultural quality of the supposedly noncultural choices of the hermits.

We learn here that using wild resources and eating them just as they are found in nature is not at all a simple, natural procedure born of instinctive wisdom. Rather, it is the result of a learning process, of acquired knowledge of the land and its resources. That knowledge is gained by gathering information and taking advantage of the teachings of those already familiar with the land in question and the uses of its resources. In the case in point the informant was an animal sent by God; there were no other men around to transmit culture to the solitary hermit. But he could not have survived without culture.

Cultural associations of this type were of long historical duration. In eighteenth-century Europe, suspended between Enlightenment rationalism and preromantic passion, the mistrust of cooks and the fascination with a simple cuisine, precultural and by and large raw, are recurrent motives in literature, as in the "naturalistic" utopia of Rousseau. The noble savage does not cook, and he is happy!

In our own time, with widespread environmentalism, such images often disclose themselves in food attitudes and behavior—so much so that in the twentieth century raw food has found an ally above suspicion in dietetic science. The discovery of vitamins has actually endowed the raw with a new symbolic aura as an image for healthy behavior: the less foods are cooked, the more they retain their nutritional value. This differs radically from the arguments implicit in the old dietetic doctrine, which was based instead on the idea of transformation, and of a long cooking process.

# Roasted and Boiled

The cultural tensions implicit in culinary preparations are such that they cannot be ideologically neutral.

Eginardo, the biographer of Charlemagne, tells us that the sovereign always enjoyed the best of health except for the last four years of his life, when he suffered from frequent fevers and eventually also from gout (he limped on one foot). Eginardo also documents the disputatious arguments that broke out, because of this illness, between the emperor and his doctors. The latter, he viewed as "particularly hateful" because they urged him to replace the roasts he was used to eating with boiled meats.

Was this simply a matter of taste? Surely not. Nor was it a matter of mere personal predilection. Behind Charlemagne's habit of eating roasts and his rejection of boiled meats, it is easy to perceive very specific cultural preferences, such as those that Lévi-Strauss has taught us to read into the ways of preparing or cooking foods.

Not only in the traditions or conventions of older societies but even in today's, the roasted and the boiled play an antithetical role on a symbolic level. They mean something very different in the usual play of opposites between culture and nature, domesticated and wild. Fraught with ambiguity, as we have already emphasized, these antitheses (even the choices in favor of "nature") are eminently "cultural." This does not take away from the fact that in the choice of foods and of cooking processes, roasting decisively remains an expression of "nature" and of the "wild," since the only means of cooking required is a fire over which the meat is cooked directly.

How else could we imagine the scenes at the end of a hunting foray such as those that filled the lives of the medieval and *ancien régime* aristocrats if not by including an animal on a spit turning over a roaring fire? For these men the pungent taste of roasted meat was a habitual experience that bordered on the commonplace, as it appears in the narration of the emperor's culinary routines. Charlemagne's daily meal, wrote Eginardo, normally consisted of four courses . . . not including the roasts "that the hunters used to skewer on the spit and which he ate with more relish than any other dish." To these, which his doctors tried in vain to discourage him from eating, the emperor was "accustomed." The Latin participial adjective *assuetus* suggests more than just habit, but also in some ways a virtual addiction—that is, a psychological dependency so difficult to overcome that it shows us how behavioral eating patterns are not only the fruit of rationally followed economic and nutritional value systems but of choices (or compulsions) tied to mental constructs and symbols of which we are the bearers and in some sense prisoners.

In contrast, boiling "mediates" through water the relationship of fire and food and necessitates the use of a container-utensil—namely, a manufactured object that typically represents "culture"—thus tending to take on symbolic meanings more directly linked to the notion of "domestication." The house, not the forest, seems the natural setting for this kind of food preparation, and peasant cuisine is more typically characteristic of it.

This has remained true up to our own time. That continuity is confirmed by all kinds of evidence, not only written but also reified (such as archeological artifacts). There have been, for example, excavations conducted on medieval sites that have revealed a precise correlation between the physical dimensions of cooking utensils and the size of the animal skeletons recovered from the same deposits. The bones, obviously, were cut down to a size allowing them to fit into these containers. The pot, suspended over an always-lit fire and protected and covered by a head ring of stone in the middle of the room, for channeling the rising smoke, was the centerpiece of this kitchen, as indeed it was in the countryside until very recent times. Even in the wall fireplaces of bourgeois houses, a pot was hung, as shown in the miniatures of the late Middle Ages (above all, the *Tacuina sanitati*) and in depictions of subsequent centuries. Monastic kitchens also gave preference to boiled or stewed preparations (of meats, to be sure, but above all of vegetables and greens).

The symbolic values attributed to boiled foods—domesticated culture, a "gentle" relationship to food—took root in a reality of lower cost and higher yield (values dear to the peasant world but alien to the aristocratic mentality). Cooking in a pot, rather than directly on the fire, also meant not wasting the nutritive juices of meats, but holding them in and concentrating them in the water. The broth obtained in this way could be reused for other preparations, together with new meats, cereals, vegetables, and greens. In the use of the pot it is hard to mistake the motive of economy and conservation. Besides, water was all but indispensable when it came to cooking salted meats (as were, for the most part, those eaten by the peasants), whereas fresh meat was a sign of social privilege.

The dialectic of roasting and boiling is also implicitly one of gender. The pot boiling on the domestic hearth enters into the arena of female competence. Stoking the fires to roast meat is more often than not a "man's" specialty, actually better expressed as virile or masculine, which calls up images of brutal simplicity, as well as mastery over natural forces.

In all their ambiguity, these images continue to condition our ways of thinking about our relationship to food. The open-air barbecue, which parades rough gestures and primitive macho manners, is a vestige of ancient powers that even today seem antithetical to the complexity of elaborate and domestic cuisine. You can now pick up picnic equipment at the supermarket, and ready-to-use charcoal has replaced the search for wood and kindling to build the fire. Still, in the outdoor fire we maintain the illusion of creating and reestablishing a strong bond with nature.

The lifestyle of the hunter, or perhaps even of the cowboy, has not lost its fascination. That lifestyle can even enter into national identity when consciously assimilated into the ideals of a society, such as the American society, which may indeed admire European cuisine but cannot help regarding it as excessively sophisticated.

# Pleasure and Health

The use of fire combines with the development of kitchen procedures not only to improve the taste of foods but also to enhance safety, hygiene, and health. The interdependence of cuisine and dietetics remains a given. We could call this the very basis of food culture itself, which we could trace back to the time when man first learned to use fire to cook his food. This simple act surely was, from its very beginning, intended to make food more hygienic, as well as more flavorful. Thus, we can state with some certainty that dietetics was born with cooking.

With time this relationship became more deliberate and elaborate, evolving into a science of dietetics within the theory and practice of medicine. This took place in ancient Greece, where, between the fifth and fourth centuries B.C., Hippocrates of Cos founded a school of thought that survived in Europe for several millennia. Analogous developments can be readily discerned in civilizations like the Indian and Chinese, which evolved medical and philosophical systems rigorously tied to culinary practices; and these were systems not lacking in significant links to the Western tradition.

Premodern medicine is often labeled "Galenic" in honor of the Roman physician Galienus (second century A.D., whose teaching, which took up and developed the Hippocratic theories, remained alive until the seventeenth century and even beyond.

Galienus's medicine was founded on a fundamental principle, from which were derived most of the ideas and practices dealing with the care of the body: Every living being—man, animal, or plant—possesses its own particular "nature" determined by a combination of four factors, paired off two by two: *hot and cold; dry and moist*. These in turn are the expressions of the four elements which constitute the universe: fire, air, earth, and water.

Man can call himself healthy when the various elements of his body combine in a stable and balanced manner. If one of the elements dominates another, because of a temporary state of illness, because of old age (the young being hotter and moister, the elderly colder and drier), because of the climate and environment in which they live, or because of their line of business, or for whatever reason, it becomes imperative to restore the balance with expedient strategies, first among them the control of food. For example, if one were stricken with an illness that made him too "moist," he would then do better to choose "dry" foods, and vice versa. The individual in good health, on the other hand, would do better to eat a balanced diet, consisting of foods that are said to be "temperate."

It is precisely here that cuisine enters the picture. Cuisine is to be understood as the art of manipulation and skillful combination, given that perfectly balanced foods do not exist in nature. An intervention therefore becomes necessary to correct and thereby to restore to the equipoise of moderation those natural qualities of the food product (classified according to a complicated table of intensity or "degrees"). If a certain food is unbalanced by "heat," it needs to be modified and steered back toward "cold." Or else the "hot" food should be accompanied by "cold" ingredients, chosen according to two principal lines of intervention: the techniques of cooking and the modalities of food pairings.

Onto these bases is grafted the idea, typical of ancient, medieval, and Renaissance culture, that cuisine is basically an "artifice." As might seem obvious, it was also an art of combining that had not yet appreciated the full nature of products, but rather sought to rectify or correct that nature.

In this perspective what becomes clear, first of all, are indications of how to cook foods, detailed by texts found both in recipe collections and in dietetic guides. A precise correlation, we learn, must exist between the kind of meat (of differing categories according to type, age, and sex of the animal) and the way that meat is to be cooked. If the meats are "dry," better add water, that is, boil them; if they are "moist," it is preferable to dry or roast them. "Venison must be eaten boiled or stewed," wrote the sixth-century doctor Antimo; "roasts, if they come from a young deer, are good, but if the deer is old, they are heavy." Advice that became proverbial was that "an old hen makes good soup!"

Similar criteria orient and guide the pairings—another strong point in ancient and medieval nutrition, which determined many choices in the gastronomic field. These pairings later entered into general usage lasting even until today: Why does one eat cheese with pears and melon with prosciutto? The pairings recall premodern "nutritionism," which was fairly mistrustful of many kinds of fruit (among them pears and melons) judged excessively "moist" and dangerous for one's health. The function of cheese, or of prosciutto (both "dry"), was "to dry" the nature of the products they accompany. Alternatively, one can use salt, the drying substance par excellence (which in France is often sprinkled on melon). But these fruits are not only "moist" but also dangerously "cold." Accompanying the melon with a fortified sweet wine (in France, often a glass of port) brilliantly resolves the problem. As for pears, in most cases on medieval and Renaissance menus they are served cooked in wine (this custom too becoming traditional and maintained to this day).

The "Galienus cook," in whose professionalism is combined the art of cuisine and medical wisdom, also devoted extraordinary care to sauces. Served opportunely side by side with meats and fish, the precise purpose of a sauce is to temper such foods, making them at the same time digestible and tasty. Both desiderata (taste and health) remain conjoined, since an essential principle of premodern cuisine and nutrition is that foods, to be well assimilated by the organism, must also awaken the digestive juices through the pleasure of eating.

Garlic sauces, writes Bartolomeo Sacchi, a.k.a. the humanist Platina, in his treatise *On Honest Pleasure and Good Health* (mid-fifteenth century) are to be used with tough and fatty meats "to make them more digestible and to stimulate the appetite." Desire may constitute the perceptible sign of an unexpressed need. That the pleasure of satisfying that desire may represent the path to physical health is an idea so widely shared that it borders on the obvious.

"What is most pleasing to the taste is best for the digestion," wrote Maino de'Maineri, a fourteenth-century physician from Milan, author of a dietetic treatise, which in numerous ways resembles a cookbook or recipe collection thanks to the many practical suggestions dealing with the cooking of foodstuffs, the ways of preparing them, and their various possible combinations. Not for nothing did an entire chapter of Maino's *Regimen*, devoted to sauces, circulate as an autonomous text with the title *De Saporibus* ("On Tastes").

Reciprocally, it is not difficult to discover signs of medical precepts in recipe collections, since medicine and cookery are two aspects of the same corpus of knowledge. The bean, wrote Platina, is hot and moist, but its noxiousness can be tempered with a sprinkle of oregano, pepper and mustard, and an accompaniment of a dry wine.

These are generally shared rules and practices, because dietetics speaks the same language as cuisine, a language compatible with—actually completely submersible into—that of the senses. Hot and cold, dry and moist are not abstract categories but theoretical constructs based on sensory experience. Therefore, this popularizing language encapsulates the entire social spectrum, linking, though with different degrees of awareness, learned treatises and rustic traditions, scientific speculation and down-to-earth daily practices.

Not only readers of Maino and Platina but even the lowly customers of the tavern knew full well that pears, peaches, or cherries went well with cheese. The meals on the menu eaten at the Albergo della Stella in Prato between 1395 and 1398—punctiliously documented by the owners of the inn—ended with cooked pears and cheese (or, according to the season, with cheese and cherries in May, and cheese and peaches in September). This is a valuable bit of evidence, because it concerns clients of all social classes and lists individual dishes on the menu requested by them. There is really not a great disparity between the culinary culture of these coach-house customers and that of a great prince like Filippo Maria Visconti, Lord of Milan, who, according to the testimony of his biographer, Pier Candido Decembrio, ended his meal with "some pears and apples cooked in cheese."

Once the kind of cooking preparation had been chosen and the combinations decided, the third strategic action of nutritional good health was no longer up to the cook but to the maître d'—or steward (formerly called the *scalco*): to bring out the dishes during the meal, according to a sequence that favored good assimilation or good digestion.

"What things should be eaten first?" is a problem to which Platina devotes a useful chapter of his treatise, as well as numerous observations within its individual chapters and subsections. "In choosing foods one must observe a certain order, since at the beginning of the meal one can eat without trepidation and with greater pleasure those things that stimulate the stomach and offer light and moderate nourishment." Certain kinds of apples and pears, lettuces come to mind, and "everything both raw and cooked dressed in oil and vinegar." As regards fruits, the advice given is to open the meal with the sweet and flavorful kind and to end it with the tart and astringent. When dealing with apples, pears, pomegranates, mulberries, and blackberries, this is indeed the rule to follow. Melons and peaches are to be accompanied by good wine, "to prevent their rotting" in the stomach. Among the citrus fruit one must choose the sweetest; should these be too bitter, they can be sweetened with sugar. To begin with salads, oil, and vinegar is another possibility, recommended in the sixteenth century by Costanzo Felici, a botanist and gastronome from the Marches.

The dynamic of pleasure–health, which contemporary iconography often tends to perceive in conflicting terms, was thought of as an indissoluble union in premodern cultures, within which the two elements of pleasure and health reinforce each other. The idea that pleasure could be healthy, that "what is pleasurable is beneficial is a core idea in ancient and medieval dietetics.

Seen the other way around, "the rules of health" are first of all dietary rules, rules understood not in the sense of *restrictions* (as the usual distorted meaning of the word "diet" prevalent in everyday language today would indicate), but rather in the *construction* of a gastronomic culture. The methods of cooking the ingredients, the criteria for combinations of foods, the sequence of courses within the meal are all variables closely connected to dietetic principles. This obviously does not mean that every food preparation is calculated with health in mind. Contradictory situations can also arise when other motivations, such as social prestige, or simple gluttony, enter into play. But, generally speaking, dietetic science and the art of gastronomy move in close symbiosis, especially because, as we have seen, they speak the same language.

Beginning with the seventeenth and eighteenth centuries, dietetic science began to speak a different language, one based on chemical analysis and experimental physics. The categories of hot and cold, and of dry and moist, developed by Greek and Latin medicine beginning with Aristotelian physics, allowed for a continuous, and one might say, a natural interchange between daily experience and conceptual exposition, between culinary practices based on taste and discussions of the nutritional value of foods.

The new dietetics introduced concepts, formulas, and language no longer tied to sensorial experience: Who knows the flavor of carbohydrates or the taste of vitamins? From this was born an important bifurcation, or gap, that we have difficulty bridging. Despite this, today as yesterday, dietetic science profoundly affects our way of gathering at the table. The relationship of pleasure and health, developed during a primitive era with the first experiments in cooked foods, continues to be a fundamental constant in the cultural experience of *homo edens* (man the consumer of good food).

# The Pleasure and the Duty of Choice

# Taste Is a Cultural Product

Food is neither good nor bad in the absolute, though we have been taught to recognize it as such. The organ of taste is not the tongue, but the brain, a culturally (and therefore historically) determined organ through which are transmitted and learned the criteria for evaluations. Therefore, these criteria vary in space and in time. What in one epoch is judged positively, in another can change meaning; what in one locale is considered a tasty morsel, in another can be rejected as disgusting. Definitions of taste belong to the cultural heritage of human society. As there are differing tastes and predilections among different peoples and regions of the world, so do tastes and predilections evolve over the course of centuries.

But how can one presume to reconstruct the "taste" in and of food for eras so distant from our own?

The question in reality hearkens back to two distinct meanings of the term *taste*. One of these is taste understood as flavor, as the individual sensation of the tongue and palate—an experience that is by definition subjective, fleeting, and ineffable. From this point of view the historical experience of food is irretrievably lost. But taste can also mean knowledge (*sapere* vs. *sapore*): it is the sensorial assessment of what is good or bad, pleasing or displeasing. And this evaluation, as we have said, begins in the brain before it reaches the palate.

From this perspective, taste is not in fact subjective and incommunicable, but rather collective and eminently communicative. It is a cultural experience transmitted to us from birth, along with other variables that together define the "values" of a society. Jean-Louis Flandrin coined the expression "structures of taste" as suitable for emphasizing the collective and shared "values" of this experience. And it is clear that this second dimension of the problem, which does not coincide with the first but in large measure conditions it, can be investigated historically by examining the memoirs and the archeological finds constituting the traces that every past society has left behind.

Let us take medieval and Renaissance society. What are we able to learn from the documents surrounding the patterns of taste and food consumption from a thousand or even five hundred years ago? What variants stand out in comparison to today?

To a retrospective investigation moving from today in quest of the medieval, it seems suddenly clear that our concept of cuisine and the system of tastes that seem to us so "naturally" preferable are very different from those that for a long time (and not only in the Middle Ages but as recently as two centuries ago) were judged as good and therefore to be sought out.

Today's Italian and European cuisine has a predominantly analytical character. By that I mean that it tends to differentiate tastes: sweet, salty, bitter, sour, spicy . . . reserving for each of these an autonomous space, either in a specific food or in the sequence of the meal.

Tied to this is the notion that insofar as possible, cuisine must respect the natural flavor of each food component. The quest is for a flavor that is different each time and unique, thanks to its having been maintained as specifically distinct from others. But these simple rules do not constitute a global archetype of an "Ur-cuisine," always extant and consistent unto itself. These rules are the fruit of a minor revolution that took place in France between the seventeenth and eighteenth centuries.

"Cabbage soup should taste of cabbage, leeks of leek, turnips of turnip," Nicola de Bonnfons suggested in his *Letters to Household Managers* (mid-seventeenth century). In appearance it is an innocent enough declaration, disconcerting in its banality, but in fact this notion overturned ways of thinking and eating that had been firmly held for centuries.

Renaissance taste, as well as medieval taste, and going back even further, that of ancient Rome, had indeed developed a model of cuisine based principally on the idea of artifice and on the blending of flavors. Both the preparation of individual foods and their placement within the meal answered to a logic more *synthesizing* than analytical: to bind together more than to separate. This also corresponded to the rules of dietetic science, which considered a "balanced" food as that which contained in itself all the nutritional qualities, each displayed in turn, rendered by perceptibly distinct flavors. The perfect food was considered that in which all the tastes (therefore all the virtues) would be simultaneously present. Specific to this end, the cook was obliged to alter the products, changing their characteristics in a more or less radical fashion.

A typical example of this culture is the sweet-salty taste dynamic characterizing many of the medieval and Renaissance food preparations. Or take the bittersweet, a mixture of sugar and citrus fruits (thanks to two new products brought to Europe by the Arabs), which reinterpreted and refined the old combination of honey and vinegar already typical of Roman cuisine. These tastes have not completely vanished, however, since even today they can be found in more conservative European culinary traditions, as in the Germanic countries and, more generally, those of eastern Europe.

Think of blueberry jam, the pears and apples used as garnishes for meats, and especially for game: that is medieval cuisine. To remain in Italy, recall products like Cremona mustard (chutney) which blends the sharpness of spices with the sweetness of sugar: that is medieval cuisine. Think of casseroles or timbales of macaroni (a pastry crust filled with a salted dough flavored with sweet spices), traditional in various Italian regions and cities. Think of pepper and of sugar in *pan-pepato* (pepper bread) and of other Christmas sweets. To wander further afield, think of the sweet and sour in Chinese cooking, of the honey-crusted pigeon in the Moroccan tradition: that too is medieval cuisine. This cuisine of flavor contrasts is a quest for balance, for a zero degree in which the distances between tastes are cancelled out.

This "structure of taste," strongly correlated with dietetic science, and in some way as well with the philosophy and worldview of each age, has been totally transformed in Europe during the last two centuries—first in France, then in Italy. This structure constitutes the greatest barrier for us to understanding a reality so different from our own.

Another basic characteristic of premodern gastronomy, one that keeps it remote from our own, is the extremely sparing use of fats. The cuisine of half a millennium ago was fundamentally *lean*. To assemble sauces, the inevitable accompaniment to meat and fish, one used above all acidic ingredients such as wine, vinegar, citrus juice, and the juice of sour grapes—ingredients to be bound with soft bread crumbs, liver, almond milk, and eggs.

Fatty sauces, based on oil and butter, are far more familiar to our taste. By that I mean mayonnaise, béchamel, and all the gravies typical of nineteenth- and twentieth-century bourgeois cooking. These are modern creations, dating from the seventeenth century, which have profoundly transformed the taste and appearance of foods.

If we want to propose a contemporary parallel to medieval European cooking, I suggest that we look rather at the sauces of Japanese or Southeast Asian cuisines, which are lean and, to be precise, completely without dairy products or oil.

Cooking techniques follow this tendency to superimpose and to blend flavors, rather than to separate and deconstruct them. Boiling, roasting, frying, stewing, brazing, were obviously differing ways of cooking. But they were also, in many cases, different stages of the same cooking process, superimposed or so to speak "cumulative," like successive phases in the preparation of the same dish. In some cases this might have been to answer practical exigencies: preliminary boiling of meats (a process that remained in use until at least the eighteenth century) also helped to preserve the meats until, with a few finishing touches, they were later worked into more complex dishes. Boiling might also have served to tenderize meats. But, like all gastronomic choices, it all ultimately came down to a matter of taste: by combining various cooking techniques, one could obtain particular flavors and special textures.

One element that was very well known to ancient and medieval sensibilities, so much more accustomed to a *tactile* relationship with foods than our own, lay both in the gustatory approach and in the physical relationship to foods directly handled (literally) without intermediaries, thus reducing to a minimum the use of cutlery. Only the spoon was really necessary—for liquid foods.

The fork appeared either as a form of extreme (and long controversial) refinement of the habits of social etiquette, or as a sheer necessity when approaching foods like piping hot and slippery pasta, which were difficult to manage with the hands. It is no accident that the development of the fork first took place in Italy rather than elsewhere, because it was above all in Italy, and as early as the final centuries of the Middle Ages, that the culture of pasta took on a prominence unknown elsewhere. But for meat-based foods, even well into the modern era, the use of the fork continued to seem unnatural and hygienically debatable.

Finally, our relationship to food was radically transformed by the spread toward mid-nineteenth century of the so-called service à la russe. This was the custom of serving guests a succession of courses preselected and the same for all. "Service à la russe" is the norm today and seems to us somehow obvious.

The model adhered to until then was quite different, rather more like what we still find today in China, in Japan, and in other countries of the world. Courses are served on the table *simultaneously*, and it was up to each guest to choose his food and to sequence dishes according to his own taste. In simple meals there would be one dish; in more complex and prestigious meals, a series of hot (kitchen-prepared) dishes or a cold (buffet) succession of dishes, the number depending on the lavishness of the banquet. In any case it was up to individual dinner guests to choose according to their own *pleasure* and their own *need*—two notions that, as we have seen, premodern dietetic science tended to bring together, interpreting desire as revealing a physiological need.

# Digression: Playing at "Historical Cuisine"

A fashion of recent years that has spread everywhere in Italy and throughout Europe is that of "historical" cuisine, re-created preferably in buildings that are equally "historical," to satisfy the curiosity of tourists and to make the cultural entrepreneurs happy.

"Medieval" cuisine, above all others, is quite the rage these days. I put it between quotation marks, because, in so many cases, the "Middle Ages" is not a true historical referent but an evocative name, transporting one to a "past" that is indefinable in its chronological outlines.

The historian cannot help but ask himself, does all this make sense? Can one *reconstruct* the culinary taste of an era apparently so near to us that it surrounds us everywhere with its vestiges and yet remains so remote in its basic "aesthetic" points of reference?

The key challenge is to delineate the boundary between mere inclusion and creative adaptation, reconstruction and rethinking, and between philological study of texts and practical hands-on work in the kitchen. Let us state it without ambiguity: to identify this boundary is difficult a priori, and even more so, it means starting cold, so to speak. Only the sensibility and experience of those who do serious work on the subject can define the limits of history and romance properly, even if precariously. I take it as a given that although one can study and reconstruct the gastronomic culture of past centuries somewhat credibly, it seems to be wishful thinking to effect a transition to the practical plane of present experience, with its individual taste sensations.

The material object has changed—today's products are no longer those of a thousand years ago, even if they have the same name. More important, the subject has changed as well: consumers are no longer the same, and their sensorial training is very different. This predicament is, to say the least, desperate for whoever presumes to achieve a "historically" plausible result. It is somewhat like hearing fourteenth-century *Ars nova* or the innovative melodies of Guillaume de Machaut, in the philological reconstitution of the music of curators and connoisseurs of ancient music. No matter how hard we try, we do not succeed in driving out of our minds our experience of hearing Bach, Mozart, and Beethoven (or Stravinsky or Schoenberg, for that matter). So we cannot relive the experience of those who centuries ago regarded the music of the *Ars nova* and Machaut as an avant-garde experience. On an intellectual level, *full immersion* in the past can in some way work; on a subjective, emotional level, it remains technically impossible.

In fact, from the point of view of subjective affect, I would not at all presume to assert that remaining philologically faithful to the text would be the best way to reconstitute the *sensations* of a particular era. Even the opposite might occur: the maximum degree of adjustment and flexible adaptation—expertly controlled—could turn out in the end to be more authentic than slavish fidelity to the formal text.

One example only: The mortar and pestle are very different in their function from an electric mixer, and very different too are the textures and consistencies that one obtains with the two utensils. But in the framework of *our* experience, the mixer is the tool to use if you want to grind finely, as was the mortar during the Middle Ages. These two sensorial experiences, objectively distant, might be perceived to coincide on a subjective plane. In any case, we shall never know.

And what applied to techniques applies all the more to tastes and flavors. What we today consider the "overly spiced" foods of the medieval period were not so for the men of that earlier time. The same holds true for ways of approaching and handling food. To eat with one's hands, as we ought to do if we are to imitate fully the medieval usage, no longer belongs to our experience (although one does find it in other food cultures, such as that which serves Moroccan couscous—North Africa can once again be imagined as still living a medieval reality). Today we are no longer adept at it, or in any case eating with our hands implies a curious exoticism. In the Middle Ages the practice was normal; for us now it no longer is in our mores (notwithstanding the exception to the rule that we experience so extensively today at McDonald's, whose success incidentally would also seem to owe much to retrieving atavistic and repressed historical experiences).

In any case we shall have to content ourselves with approximations, and with curiosity destined to remain skin deep, even if intellectually alert and well researched. It is a bit like our traveling to far-off lands and seeking to understand, even if we obviously cannot fully share, cultures different from our own.

The proposition could be that of "playing at historical cuisine," respecting a few rules (there is no game without rules), but without falling into the self-importance of the philological reconstruction of a recipe, revived in all its purported "authenticity." This game, besides giving us inauthentic emotional thrills, would in so many instances not even be feasible. Let us not forget that cookbooks often omit the measured quantities of the ingredients—omissions due not to an innate lack of precision but to the fact that the recipes were intended for a readership of experts, if not always of professional cooks.

Above all, reconstituting the "authentic" recipe would be a foolhardy ambition. It would be contrary not only to the art of cooking, which is first of all an art of invention, but also to the more authentic spirit of a historical tradition (yes, for once, an authentic one), which we would want to use as a point of reference for our experiments. The incredible number of variants found in medieval recipe collections for dishes with the same name are not only expressions of regional or local individuations. They are important of themselves in the definition of types of cuisine, for these variants become the metaphor for the basic principle that every fine cook ought to follow: "This being said," reads a fourteenth-century Italian text, "a worthy cook will be learned in all matters, in harmony with the diversity of animal and vegetable kingdoms and will be able to vary and flavor foods as he deems proper."

# Taste Is a Product of Society

If all food-related behaviors face a moment of necessary choice, the mechanisms by which this choice is accomplished are diverse indeed. If we want to speak of "types of taste," how these are formed and are modified over time, then a question we cannot refrain from asking is: *whose* taste?

It is of course clear that hunger for the many and abundance for the few hardly lead to the same choices. If all had the right to convert to pleasure their need for daily sustenance, the modalities for calibrating the fulfillment of that need would be highly varied.

The anthropologist Marvin Harris, advocate of a strictly utilitarian materialism, maintains that food choices made by the peoples and by individuals are always determined according to a more or less conscious calculation of the resulting advantages and disadvantages. Ultimately, the differing food regimens, not excluding those that make room for cannibalism, would be the most practical and economical possible, historically, under certain conditions, since in every society the preferred foods would always be those "that tip the scales toward practical benefits compared to the scale of costs." Hence nutritional customs; hence the assessment of certain foods as "good" and of others as "bad."

"Good to eat," or rather, *fit to eat*, became historically, according to Harris, "fit for thought," the positive cultural value. But all this works—and that within certain limits—only if we speak of the lower classes and of their never adequately satisfied hunger. It is clear that *their* habits and thus in the final analysis *their* tastes are determined by the ease with which they obtain a product, by its suitability for preservation and processing, by its capacity *to fill the belly*, thereby alleviating the distressing bite of hunger. This can explain the popular taste for starches: wheat, legumes, chestnuts, all comfort foods that *fill*; so too can be explained the more recent taste for pasta, or for potatoes.

Of course, it is not always stated that food *habits* correspond to individual *tastes*. Jean-Louis Flandrin has insisted on the following: it is one thing to eat a food sporadically, or even regularly; it is quite another to appreciate it. The element of necessity can in many cases bridge the gap between the two. European peasants who for centuries ate dark bread baked with cheaper grains such as rye, spelt, or orzo, certainly developed a physiological affinity for this kind of food. That does not take away from the fact that they may always have wanted to eat white wheat bread like the lords and the city-dwellers. Only the culinary anhedonia and boredom of rich urban residents could have transformed the poor folk's dark bread into an elite food. By promoting it for greengrocers' shops and specialty food stores, these urban consumers created new images of a past that had never actually existed, and of a blissful and uncorrupted rural life that the peasants themselves had never known.

And here it would be difficult to measure how genuine—in their taste buds, that is—might be the appreciation of rich consumers for these rustic foods. The suspicion is that they eat these foods because the *idea* that they have formed of these foods makes them feel good. The trajectory of Harris's specific argument, that is, from habit to taste, from eating to conceptualization, would on this matter at least seem to be reversed.

Actually, if we reverse the social-reference perspective and move from the context of poverty to that of wealth, the mechanism of formation of taste itself seems reversed. The object of desire is no longer the food available in abundance but the one that is rare; not the food that fills you and alleviates hunger but the one that whets the appetite, inviting you to eat more.

In the sixteenth century, certain hedonists, to cite but one curious example, acquired the habit of eating salad halfway through the meal in order to rekindle their waning appetites. Since this "whets and stimulates the appetite," these people, clearly "too greedy for food," violated the normal dietetic rules, which suggested serving the salad at the beginning of the meal. The quotation is from the Marches botanist Costanzo Felici, who does not fail to condemn the behavior of these gluttons.

As for the allure of rare foods, the most striking example is that of spices, which in the Middle Ages enjoyed extraordinary success on the table of the ruling classes. They were progressively shunned during the seventeenth century, however, when their greater availability at the market, with a resulting decline in prices, made them accessible to a larger clientele. At this juncture spices were no longer indicators of social distinction. The elites sought new upscale bases of distinction: butter, pastry, or even fresh garden vegetables, the latter a "retrieval" of peasant food models culturally analogous, in its ambiguity, to today's "alternatives" in the dietary regimens of the poor.

The *anti*-low-cost budgetary trend would thus seem to be an important motor in the process of the formulation of taste in the upper classes, for the simple reason that, as Isidor of Seville wrote about the bean in the seventh century, "anything available in abundance is vile." Another good example is that of fresh fruit, a particularly delicate and perishable product, which for a long time was linked to images of luxury and riches. In particular, during the centuries of the late Middle Ages and of the early modern era, fruit was in fashion on the tables of the wealthy, marking a typical characteristic of "aristocratic gourmandise." And we must keep in mind that in this case, unlike others, the food choice clashed with the medical advice of the time. Actually, the contemporary dietetic science was very suspicious of fruit, then widely considered a source of cold humors and of noxious moisture, bad for the digestive process. Nonetheless, the fashion spread. Imagination, as so often happens, won out over reason.

# From the Geography of Taste
# to the Taste of Geography

"To eat geographically," to know or express a culture of a specific region through cuisine, local produce, products, recipes, seems to us absolutely "natural." Among the differing forms of identity suggested and communicated by food-related customs, *terroir* may be the one that today seems to us most obvious. But this well-established commonplace, even cliché, according to which the cuisine of a region would be an ancient, indigenous, atavistic reality, is based on a misunderstanding, one deserving a pause for serious consideration.

First of all, we ought to distinguish between *produce* and *dishes* (the individual recipes) on the one hand, and on the other, *cuisine* (understood as an ensemble of dishes and of rules). Local dishes linked to local produce clearly have always existed. From this point of view, all food is by definition "local," that is, of the *region,* especially if we think of popular culture, which is more directly tied to local resources. But even on a higher plane, even when the decisive variant of the marketplace enters into play, attention devoted to products labeled as "of specific origin" is not an innovation.

One could cite as examples an endless number of authors and leading figures to show to what extent awareness of *terroir,* of local conditions and resources, has always constituted an essential given of food culture. Evidence ranges chronologically from Archestrato di

Gela, who in the fourth century B.C. listed the kinds of fish one could catch in the Mediterranean and suggested for each species the area where its quality was at its best, to Ortensio Lando, who in his *Commentary on the most famous and prodigious things about Italy and other places* (1548), described the gastronomic and enological specialties of different cities and regions of the Italian peninsula.

The fact is that this knowledge of a cluster of local determinants did not really fit into "regional culture," or into a resolution to "eat geographically" (an expression coined by French geographer Jean-Robert Pitte). The goal of the premodern "gastronome" was not to fit into a given culture, to know an area through its flavors, but rather to bring together all experiences, to gather onto one's own table all possible regions into a kind of universal banquet. Archestrato, who catalogued the fish from all regions, wanted all of them together on his table. Imperial Rome was proclaimed by the writers of the time the world's biggest emporium, one where all so-called local products were simultaneously presented with the widest possible variety of offerings, aiming directly at transcending local parameters or limitations of *terroir* and going beyond the region. This syncretistic culture meant, precisely, that the table was by and large a universal place. According to each person's possibilities, from the table of the emperor and gradually descending the social ladder to the plebeians, the primary objective remained that of gathering all kinds of products from all kinds of places into this magical central arena, the table set for a feast.

In the Middle Ages the markets of Bologna and Milan were renowned not so much for the local foods found there as for their capacity to define themselves as places of interterritorial, interregional, and international exchange. The Paris market for centuries was organized in the same way and thrived on this very same image.

The same holds true for "dishes"—for local specialties. Like the products themselves, these may always have existed as bound to the region, the resources, and the local traditions. But there also emerges historically an apparently incongruous objective: The goal was not yet set to distinguish specialties in order to use them as identifying signs of different cultures, but rather to gather them together, to mix, and to blend them. This is evident in the tradition of antiquity as well as in medieval fourteenth- and fifteenth-century cookbooks that are compilations of recipes of the most varied provenance (or at least of differing attribution), such as "Rome," "Treviso," "Puglia," and "Lombardy."

In his fifteenth-century recipe collection, the most famous Italian cook of his time, Maestro Martino, catalogued "Roman style cabbage," "Bolognese Tart," "Eggs Florentine style," and many other "local" recipes. Setting aside the plausibility of each individual attribution, which could be the fruit of chance, circumstance, or confusion, there is no doubt whatsoever that what was sought by this culture was above all to unite and combine different experiences—Italian, but not only Italian, also German, French, Catalonian, English. This type of what was by and large a "universal" cuisine could be found in all European countries. There was an obvious affinity of tastes and flavors among the recipes from Italian books and those from beyond the Alps.

In summary, the dishes and local products of the Middle Ages, as was the case in antiquity and later in the Renaissance, did not have as their purpose the enhancement of the value of regional cuisines (insofar as they existed). Only with the passage of time, and very slowly at that, did such positive attention to *terroir* or regionalism begin to grow.

The inversion of the trend could be felt when the season of medieval and Renaissance universalism drew to a close. At that time national identities began to define themselves, and within those emerged (but it would be better to say "were built") regional identities. Pride in this identity increased above all between the eighteenth and nineteenth centuries, when recipe books referring to the cuisines of Piedmont, Lombardy, Cremona, Macherata, and Naples appeared in Italy.

The *Modern Apicius* of Francesco Leonardi (1790) may represent the first organic attempt to gather together the regional customs of the nation. The fact remains, however, that this collection still has very few regional recipes, if by "regional" we mean the types of local cuisine recognized as such today.

Regionalism as a system was, in this period of time, a reality in progress. An important means of transmission was the cookbook published in 1891 by Pellegrino Artusi, *Science in the Kitchen and the Art of Good Eating*, a work that had an extraordinary success, with dozens of editions printed over more than a century. It ultimately became (along with *Pinocchio*) one of the most enduring best-sellers of Italian literature.

The declared purpose of Artusi's book was to unite Italy as a culinary "state," whereas at the time Italy had only recently been united as a political entity. To that end the recipe collection combines, blends, and transforms the fragments of local culture in order to make them more widely known to the urban middle class of a newly unified country well on the way to nationhood. Artusi does not always "discover" local traditions; often it is he who creates them, or invents them, shaping and adapting them to an average taste that he himself had so largely created. As Piero Camporesi has written, the project of Italian culinary unification pursued by Artusi worked rather better than the project of linguistic unification initiated by Manzoni!

But unification (and therefore, in perspective, a certain standardization of tastes and patterns of consumption) took place through greater knowledge and appreciation of local peculiarities, individuating the different cultures—the different Italies—under the emblem of intellectual inquiry, knowledge, and mutual respect. Of course, not all regions are equally represented in Artusi's cookbook, and certain zones are completely missing. Nonetheless, within these significant limitations, Artusi's was a winning choice, since it is in fact along this line that are revealed today the most highly appreciated and skillfully formulated trends of Italian national gastronomy.

Moreover, this selection fits perfectly within the cultural tradition of the country. For example, Bartolomeo Scappi, in the sixteenth century, proposed to the different and more limited public of aristocratic courts a model of "Italian" cuisine from a very privileged vantage point, since he worked as personal chef to Pope Pius V in the Vatican. He too had in mind a cross-regional and intercity dimension of comparison and linkage among differing realities.

This "regionalism" (let us rather say, this local dimension, which forms around the cities and their surrounding regions, or, as they formally call them, their "territories") is what constitutes the power of Italian cuisine today. This "regionalism" makes *la cucina italiana* not only competitive but altogether more up-to-date than other cuisines such as that of the French, historically documented and founded on a centralized, unified, "national" or nationwide model of culinary rules and principles. The weakness of Italy as a nation, of "Italia-nazione," has over time become a strength.

Thus the "taste of geography" does not belong to the past. It was only in the course of the last two centuries that a true cultural transformation, albeit a slow one, began to reverse the standards of critical evaluation. The historical moment for the development of cuisines that today we call "regional" (mistakenly attributing them to historical archetypes that never existed) was the nineteenth century, that is, to be precise, the era of industrialization. Though that might seem a

paradox, it is anything but. The beginning of the process of standardization and, potentially, of the globalization of markets and of food
models has prompted in reaction a new attention to local cultures.
The invention of "systems," which we like to label regional cuisines,
is based on fragments that have been delivered to us by history. It
cannot be said that these cuisines were born out of nothing, because
local differences have always existed; however, terroir as an *idea* and
as a *positive given* is a new invention.

Today, terroir, or the localized and regional, constitutes a value of
absolute reference in food selections. The trendy restaurant that does
not display, as a sign of quality, an offering of cuisine linked to the terroir and to fresh market produce, does not exist. This approach, fundamentally innovative even if based on traditional elements, developed concurrently with various economic and cultural phenomena.

The first, which we have hardly mentioned, is the creation of the
standardization and certification that accompanied the development
of the food industry. In reaction, this generated its opposite, something we may hear referred to as "rediscovery" (but we ought to define this simply as "discovery") of roots—a concept we will need to
return to later.

The second is the transformation of taste, already partially changed
in the preceding centuries. If premodern cuisines showed a love of
artificial flavors, the reason is that the practitioners conceived of the
kitchen as an aggressive and invasive laboratory when it came to the
natural purity of the produce and its original unmodified flavor. But
beginning in the seventeenth to eighteenth centuries (first in France,
then in other European countries), a new culture of the natural in
taste asserted itself instead.

The third phenomenon is the weakening, with the passage from a
society of hunger to one of abundance and plenty, of a value associated with food consumption, which had always been of fundamental

importance: namely, the use of food as an instrument of social differentiation. In all traditional societies the pattern of eating is the first sign of the difference between individuals and classes. But at the moment when food became a widespread commodity, this food law weakened. In its stead there arose the valorization of "region" as receptacle for a new variation: "geographic food."

It would not have been possible to develop a notion like this within a society and an ideology as rigorously class-oriented as that of premodern Europe. In the Middle Ages no one could have thought of a "regional food" because "region" is a notion that abolishes or in any case weakens social distinctions. When the paradigm of cuisine became "space," anyone (at least in theory) could occupy that space: the lord, the city-dweller, or the peasant. To privilege the notion of regional cooking from a cultural point of view signifies therefore that one has overcome the notion of food as the first and principal instrument for perpetuating social distinctions. For this reason too the concept of "regional" or "terroir" cuisine cannot be of ancient origin.

# The Paradox of Globalization

The relationship between regional cuisine and international cuisine, of "local" to "global" models of consumption, is one of the burning issues of contemporary food culture.

Regional cooking, as we have just briefly seen, has only today achieved its current iconic cultural status. That trajectory passed through danger zones like food globalization, which seemed to lead to contrary outcomes.

Here precisely lies the paradox: In a world as genuinely fragmented as were the ancient and medieval worlds, the aim was to build a *universal* model of food consumption in which all (at least all those who could afford to do so) might recognize themselves. In the global village of our own era, in contrast, values of identity, diversity, and local specificity have been established. Praise of diversity, which normally goes with the promotion of gastronomic culture, is not nostalgia for the past but above all a look at the present and the future.

If regional cuisine is essentially a modern invention, international cuisine (contrary to what one might think) has ancient roots. Roman "Mediterranean" and medieval "European" were international cuisines, potentially universal; that is, they were open to the entire known and inhabited world. Their difference with respect to current models resided not so much in the rate of "internationalization" (which then as today tended to be global) as in the breadth of the social corpus involved. For a time this was extremely limited and circumscribed, involving a minimal share of the population. Today, while still not in fact including society as a whole, a greater percentage of consumers are involved.

That is to say that the international cuisines of the past knew infinite local variations. For example, one of the most famous dishes of medieval gastronomy, "blancmange," owed its name to its all-white ingredients—rice, almond milk, the soft part of bread, chicken breast, or white flesh of fish, depending on the "lean" and "fat" days of the church calendar). This dish appears in most of the cookbooks from different regions of Italy and Europe, though with a great number of variants (some thirty-seven in all, according to J.-L. Flandrin's tally), which demonstrates that there was no single ingredient common to all thirty-seven versions handed down to us. There are some specific "national" and "regional" examples on which Flandrin himself has insisted, recognizing thereby the ancient origins of many current tastes.

In the course of the last century the tendency toward uniformity of consumer goods has grown stronger and more visible. This trend was due to the increase in exchanges or, and above all, to the work of the food industry and of the multinationals in control of world markets.

All Italians, all Europeans today, drink Coca-Cola and orange juice, eat steaks with fries, pasta, rice, and hundreds of other things. White bread, which for a time was a product for the elite (with a few well-defined exceptions), has today become the norm in most of the world's nations. Portions of meat have increased everywhere, even in Mediterranean countries traditionally linked to well-established patterns of vegetable consumption.

It is as if the food industry had created a new "universalism," this time not for the elite but rather for the masses. The trend toward globalization of consumer goods, which for a time covered a very narrow stratum of the population (the aristocrats of the courts and the city-dwelling upper bourgeois), little by little expanded to wider brackets: the petite bourgeoisie during the nineteenth century, the entire population during the twentieth. This *social expansion of globalization* should not, however, make us forget its ancient origins as cultural model.

Something of medieval universalism can be found in the proposals put forth by *worldfood* and diffused throughout the world. In a famous Paris restaurant, Alain Ducasse's SPOON, which the Red Michelin Guide defines as "planetary," you can find a menu written in English and subtitled in French, with three lists of foods among which the diner can choose freely, assembling the various courses himself. The first column lists various kinds of fish and meats, available raw, half-cooked, or cooked, prepared in every conceivable way; the second column lists the side dishes, and the third, sauces. One is reminded of medieval and Renaissance banquets. But there the selection was not made from a menu (*à la carte*) but rather from the actual foods on the table.

At SPOON the diner is invited to combine dishes in whatever way is found appealing, thereby creating hybrid dishes that might be Italo-Indiano-Nippo-Mexicano, or whatever other combination imaginable! (I am reminded here of certain books for children wherein the reader can build funny or scary pictures choosing each body "part" or feature from among numerous available variants.) Even utensils are interchangeable, and depending on one's mood of the moment, silverware or chopsticks may be used. The wines and mineral waters are from all over the world. This may perhaps be the final stage of what J.-R. Pitte calls "exchange globalization," which does not offer a single unified model of consumption like McDonald's or other worldwide food chains, but mixes together whatever could be placed on the table.

Nevertheless, distinctive differences are not at all eliminated by this wave of radical globalism. A complex geography of food customs survives within Europe—for example, in the use of beer and wine, beverages which have been shuffled about and mixed up, it is true, but which continue to have a strongly generic and geographical identification for north Central Europe (beer culture) and south Central Europe (wine culture). There even remain pockets of cider consumption, which on a map conform exactly to the geographical outlines projected during the Middle Ages: southern England and northern France. While still within the framework of cataloguing consumer foods, different local specificities remain rooted in consumer habits, above all at the working-class or "popular" level.

The uses of grains and of meat differed from region to region in the Middle Ages and continue so even today. Bread has by now become a shared common food, but only in Mediterranean countries accustomed ever since antiquity to considering it as a commodity basic to daily sustenance does bread's status remain absolutely self-evident—so much so that in whatever restaurant we frequent, bread is included in the so-called cover charge.

In many northern countries, however (exception made here for those who have adopted Mediterranean traditions), bread must be ordered expressly. The very notion of *companatico* (something eaten with bread), by assigning to other foods the function of accompaniment to bread, implicitly accords the latter a primary role. This reign of bread seems to live on (in linguistic usage and in cultural traditions) as an exclusive prerogative or at least a characteristic encountered only in the orbit of Romance languages. The term *companatico* can be found only in Latin-based languages. In the Germanic linguistic sphere, the term does not exist, because in that culture, despite every possible syncretistic measure, the point of departure of the food system (both in a material and in a mental sense) remained *other*: not bread, but meat.

There is another factor to consider: when foods and beverages resurface in the gastronomy of different countries or regions, they are never exactly the same. For example, chocolate is sweetened in various ways according to the countries involved. When Swiss chocolate is intended for the French market, it is less sweetened to satisfy a different taste desideratum. It is curious that since the Middle Ages the French have considered other nationalities, especially the Italians, as people with excessively sweet tastes, who drink too heavily fortified (sugared) wines and who use too much sugar in the preparation of foods.

A further example: coffee is drunk throughout the world, but in each country (we might say in every region) it is prepared in a different way. Coca-Cola itself, the symbol par excellence of the standardization of tastes, does not have the same flavor everywhere. Franchisees adapt the beverage to those tastes that market pollsters manage to characterize individually as tastes specific to well-defined regions.

Finally, and above all, there remains a wide divergence in the "function" of foods, in the place they occupy in the structure of meals. By "structure" I mean the fact that, as already stated, foods are not stray cells assembled haphazardly. They constitute units of meaning that perform a specific role within a food system. Pasta in Italy is almost without exception an autonomous dish. In other countries pasta is used as a side dish for meat or other foods, arousing shudders of horror in many purists. It behooves us to remind these purists that it was precisely as a side dish that pasta was originally used in the Middle Ages and Renaissance, even in Italy!

There is also the matter of beer, which in certain countries is drunk with the meal. In others, as in a traditional wine-drinking country like Spain, beer became an important player, but with a very different role. Spaniards usually drink beer *before* the meal to accompany the infinite series of *tapas* that they like to eat before sitting down at the table for the real meal itself, this time accompanied by wine. Here there is a kind of displacement of beer *outside* of the meal. In Italy, too, consumption of beer is rising, and if beer in a pizzeria is by now a ubiquitous accompaniment, it is much less so within the canonical meal of fish or meat, or with a pasta dish.

The adventure of hamburgers (another commonplace or cliché of gastronomic universalism) transported from Disneyland USA to Eurodisney, Europe, is significant indeed in demonstrating the part played by individual foods and individual dishes within the meal-structure system. The organizational model for the production of hamburgers, exported to Disney-Paris to replicate precisely and exactly what you would find in Disney-California and in Disney-Florida, did not work. And for a simple, fundamental reason: the customers at Eurodisney like hamburgers well enough, but only at mealtimes; whereas Americans eat them without any timetable whatsoever, from morning to evening. Such a scheduling situation created notable difficulties because the number of personnel hired to serve hamburgers all day long proved excessive for morning and afternoon requirements, but insufficient at noon, when people waiting for "lunch" formed endless queues.

In short, the hamburger has been accepted, but only after being adapted to fit a normal meal, becoming in this way the substitute for a sandwich or steak/frites. The foodstuff, transported from one culture to another, has been rethought and repositioned in a sequence and structure different from that of its place of origin. So it is clear that McDonald's marketing strategies are currently marked by a considerable diversification of products and flavors offered in different national and regional environments. Moreover, recent advertisement campaigns aim to create a convincing new "Mediterranean" and "vegetarian" image for the McDonald brand.

Thus, differences do not seem destined to disappear, but to be ever more accentuated in the wider competition of globalization that has heightened awareness and endowed with new meanings the cycles of discovery and rediscovery—and the invention—of food identities.

The considerations we have put forth here lead one to believe that "global" cuisine and "local" cuisine can coexist (actually, the one in some way engendered by the other), giving rise to a new, hitherto unknown model of food consumption that some sociologists have proposed calling "glocal."

Since identities, beyond being (as we have seen) variable in time are also *multiple*, the fact that I am a citizen of the world does not prevent me from being a European citizen, an Italian citizen, as well as a citizen of my city, and a member of my family, and so on. Each of these identities has its intrinsic form of expression in food; each identity, despite appearances, does not contradict the others but coexists with them.

There is no contradiction between eating at McDonald's and, for the next meal, going home for tagliatelle, or for a special dish at the local trattoria. In these two circumstances, with these two acts only apparently contradictory, so different in content and meaning from one another, we express two of the many identities that define us.

# Food, Language, Identity

# Eating Together

Eating together is typical of (even if not exclusive to) the human race. "We do not invite each other simply to eat and drink, but to eat and drink together," says one of Plutarch's characters in his *Debates among guests*. And since actions performed with others tend to forsake the simply functional level to take on a communicative value, our human socializing instinct immediately attributes *meaning* to the gestures performed while eating. So in this way we define food as an exquisitely cultural reality, not only with respect to nutritive sustenance itself but to the ways in which it is consumed, and to everything around it and pertaining to it.

Nourishment and circumstance both take on a signifying value, usually enmeshed one with another. Why? Because the language of food, unlike verbal language, cannot be left out of the concreteness of the object, nor of the intrinsic, in some way predetermined, semantic value of the means of communication. On the other hand, it can happen (as Roland Barthes observed in an essay on the "psycho-sociology of contemporary food") that "circumstance" (context) defines itself in a fashion so autonomous as to conflict with the nutritive substance of the food in question. For example, coffee, a stimulant, can take on an antithetical social value when linked to the practice of relaxation, as with the pause for the "coffee break" between two periods of work.

Barthes maintains that these "circumstantial" values are typical of the contemporary era, in which food, in a society of plenty, tends to weaken its specifically nutritional valence, thereby emphasizing instead the other, so-called accessory signifiers. But in all societies the food system is organized as a linguistic code bearing "*add-on*" values. So in some sense we could say (reversing Barthes' thesis) that the symbolic burden borne by food is all the stronger when food is viewed as a means of daily survival. Hunger certainly does not allow too many deviations from the immediacy of attending to the acquisition of resources. But it is this same preoccupation with defining a symbolic universe of great richness that depicts the table as a metaphor for life. The very etymology of the word *convivio* suggests it, identifying living together (*convivere*) with eating together. This is not an image reserved for a few chosen ones: the courtly noun and the Latin root of *convivio* should not impress us more than this.

Even the peasant family defines its own identity at the table. "To live on one bread and one wine," that is, to share food, is in medieval language an almost technical way of signifying that one belongs to the same family. Even today in different dialectal expressions, the house is identified with the food that allows the domestic community to live there together: "Let's go home" (*andiamo in casa*) in the traditional vocabulary of the Romagna region meant, "Let's go into the kitchen." On all social levels sharing a table is the first sign of membership in a group. That might be the family but also a broader community—each brotherhood, guild, or association reasserts its own collective identity at the table. Every monastic community demonstrates its affinity in the refectory where all are supposed to share the meal from which are temporarily excluded only the excommunicated—those who are tainted with some guilt.

Only the hermit eats alone, rejecting cultivated food (in favor of wild), and cooked food (in favor of raw). We have already profiled these attitudes as conscious choices of rejection of "culture." We cannot avoid pairing this generally temporary rejection of conviviality with an exemplary model of "cultural" food consumption. The ascetic hermit recovers something of the shared table if only with the sole companions admitted into his presence—wild animals. Columbanus, who toward the end of the sixth century, experienced the lonely wooded expanses of Gaul, found himself sharing wild fruit with a miraculously tame bear. Something similar happened to Yvan the knight, whose tale was told by Chrétien de Troyes in the twelfth century. Driven by an access of madness, Yvan fled the society of men and sought refuge in the forest, but even there he found himself a companion, sharing his food with a lion.

Even the aristocratic banquet was defined as a means to achieving union and solidarity around a chief or lord. But *attenzione!* Eating together does not necessarily mean all is love and harmony. If the table is the metaphor for life, it represents in a direct and exacting way both membership in a group and the relationships defined within that group.

One thinks of the differing roles among men and women in certain rural societies: the men seated at the table, the women hovering around, ready to serve, standing while eating their own meal. One recalls the separation in the monastic communities (which were extremely careful to represent in the rituals of the table the equality of rank and duty among all the religious order's brothers) between the common table and the abbot's high table, at which only high-ranking guests were seated. One thinks as well of aristocratic banquets and of the complex "geography" that characterizes and governs them. A seat is not to be assigned at random.

In more or less formalized ways, according to the era and the social and political contexts, the placement of guests serves to signal the importance and prestige of the individuals: the lord or chieftain

*[handwritten margin note: showing the power that the host has]*

95

in the center, the others at a remove inversely proportionate to the respective importance accorded them.

In the tenth century, when Liutprando of Cremona (ambassador of Otto I of Saxony) was assigned a seat unworthy of his social rank, he did not fail to protest. Something similar, according to the plot line of a fourteenth-century novella, was said to have happened to Dante Alighieri, who indignantly left the court of Naples when he was not recognized. (He had appeared in a modest poet's outfit, and was thus placed at the end of the table. He returned later, dressed sumptuously, and was given a seat befitting his fame as poet of *la Divina Commedia*.). Dante delighted in scandalizing the guests by dirtying his finery with food and wine. And since, he explained, honor had been paid not to him but to his clothes, it was only proper that they too should participate in the banquet.

One can certainly joke about such matters, but the very possibility of being playful with them reveals how serious and deeply felt they are. The symbolic power of these hierarchies will be no less potent in the modern era, with one significant variable. In an absolute monarchy it can transpire that the Lord or Chief must eat "alone" in order to establish clearly his otherness, and distinguish between his persona and his role and the courtiers who surround him.

This type of ritual persists even today when it comes to expressing formal relationships (for example, at a diplomatic or political banquet, or some public event). Separation is necessary unless the purpose is to express symbolically the *absence* of hierarchical standing, democratic nature of the group, and that of the table around which it gathers. So it is in this light that the tradition of the round table, less adapted to defining differences and hierarchies, has become especially commonplace in a "democratic" modern society. In contrast, the medieval and Renaissance table was by definition rectangular, and therefore the shape most adapted to defining distances and hierarchical relationships. (Rather exceptional, for those times, was King Arthur's Round Table, which passed into history perhaps by virtue of its uncommon shape.)

In collective dining rituals, the meaning of particular gestures resides in the elaboration of rules that serve to delineate the field of action, excluding whoever does not know them and therefore does not respect them. Monastic communities had already developed a series of rules imposing silence at table, focused attention, sober and restrained gestures, as well as moderation in taking food. In the twelfth to thirteenth centuries there appeared the first manuals teaching "table manners" to the offspring of aristocrats. It was a genre that subsequently had a great success in the early modern period with *The Courtier* by Baldassare Castiglione, *The Galateo* by Monsignor Della Casa, and many others produced in different European countries.

In a variety of ways and meanings, these are all instruments intended to define or distinguish who is *in* from who is *out*, separating the participants from the ostracized. It is for this reason that manuals of "good manners" addressed to the aristocracy always have a negative reference to the peasant who behaves badly, who "doesn't know" what the rules are, and for this reason is excluded from the lordly table. Food etiquette had become a sign of social barriers and of the impossibility of breaking them down.

Another essential aspect of eating together is that of "sharing out" food. The serving of one piece of food rather than another is never casual (unless, once again, one deliberately seeks to express an absence of hierarchy). Rather, it reproduces relationships of power and prestige within the group. On this matter we have important testimony as early as the Greek epic. In Homeric poems the guest is always offered the best piece, and in Celtic literature wild fights between feuding tribal chieftains, as well as between rival clans, were provoked around the serving up of meat. In a less bloody mode (but only because the power relationships were on the whole more rigidly structured and most often not discussed), the society at medieval and Renaissance courts singled out the carving of the meat in the banquet hall, facing the laden table, as the decisive moment of the dining ritual. This became an act with extraordinary symbolic implications from which was derived the importance, both technical and political, of the carver entrusted with this ritual.

But, as we were saying, the meaningful character of the meal is never separated from the concrete (economic and nutritional) value of the foods consumed. Therefore, it now becomes indispensable for us to establish and define a grammar of food and to decode its rules.

# The Grammar of Food

In all societies, eating habits and rituals are governed by conventions analogous to those that give meaning and stability to verbal languages themselves. This aggregate of conventions, which we shall call "grammar," informs the food system not as a simple *compilation* of products and foods, assembled in a more or less casual fashion, but rather as a structure, inside of which each component defines its meaning.

The lexicon on which this language is based obviously consists of the repertory of available animal and vegetable products, very much like the kind of morphemes (the basic units of meaning) on which are built words as well as the entire dictionary. Thus, it is a lexicon that redefines itself in the changing context of environmental, economic, social, and cultural circumstances.

A product can be obtained from the resources of the region, but also from commercial connections. It can be accessible to some, inaccessible to others (depending on the possibilities for the use of space in subsistence economies, on the availabilities of the marketplace, and on the level of prices in monetary economies). A product can be accepted or rejected, depending on individual or collective tastes or on cultural choices (I think of the rejection of meat by vegetarians, or the exclusion of certain foods and beverages in specific religious traditions).

These differences do not preclude a common language. On the contrary, they may presuppose it. When in the Middle Ages monastic regulations imposed or suggested abstinence from meat, considered at that time the most prestigious, nourishing and agreeable of foods, the apparent separation from shared values in fact brought these values back. Both used the same vocabulary with the same meaning, even if preceded by a sign of abnegation, a concomitant of the essentially penitent aspects of monastic culture. Even "specialized lexicons," reserved for a limited group of consumers, took on a distinct meaning only within a shared culture. That is why, in the Middle Ages, the consumption of spices separated the few who could afford them from the many for whom they were unaffordable. Inversely, the broadening of the spice market in the early modern era gradually reduced or even eliminated their capacity to embody "class" distinction, something that subsequently was passed on to other products.

Morphology includes the ways in which products are developed and adapted to the different demands of consumption. This takes place through culinary practices, those actions and procedures (ways of cooking and food preparation) that transform the basic morphemes into words—that is, into dishes or foods of varying uses and functions. For example, with grains one can make polentas, bread, pasta, piecrusts, focaccias: the basic ingredients are the same. What is different is the gastronomic result determined by a different type of work performed on these ingredients.

The actions as well as the processes (the recipes) always express the relationships among units of meaning. The linguistic expression "tortelli di zucca" (pumpkin tortelli), which uses the grammatical morpheme "di" (of) to designate the subordinate role of the second element in relation to the first, will in culinary practice be expressed simply by including the second within the first. And each culinary action will have its own meaning. To add to bread, pasta, or crust any kind of sweetener (honey, sugar, raisins, cooked must . . . ) will suffice to move it out of the nutritional and ordinary dimension of the dish and into the realm of a *dulcis in fondo* (end-of-the meal sweet), a dessert, a delicacy, a festive food.

*Syntax* is the structure of the sentence, which gives meaning to the lexicon and to its morphological variants. In our sphere of gastronomy it is the meal that coordinates the dishes according to criteria determining sequence, combinations, and reciprocal relationships. Just as in verbal sentences, one or more protagonists are in the center of the action, the meat or grain dish is defined variously according to cultures and social classes as well as availability.

Let us test an example, turning here to the peasant world. Polentas, like bread, generally accompany meat and greens on the plate. If meat and greens are lacking, the menu is crippled and shows that something is not working. (In the nineteenth and at the beginning of the twentieth centuries, the spread of pellagra among the northern Italian peasantry was due to the absence of any integration of the basic corn polenta with more nutritive greens or meats.) And pasta, which in medieval custom accompanied meat dishes, began, thanks to its transformation into a separate course, a brilliant career as a soloist, but then became as well the sign of a difficult food predicament. In seventeenth-century Naples the triumphant success of pasta coincided with a crisis in meat supplies in the city's markets.

Similar considerations apply to the composition of soup, which, however, did not accompany but rather incorporated meats and greens. The role of soup as an autonomous dish is therefore rather less assertive, except for significant particular differences in kind. Meat pies not only include but also actually *contain* the ingredients, lending themselves to all kinds of distinctions and to a broader range of signifiers, though these are not obviously available given the invisibility of the contents. How diverting it would be, as a late medieval cookbook recommends, to hide a golden leaf inside a pie (unbeknownst to the servants). Better still to stuff it with "nothing," as the citizens of Parma did in 1246, when, lacking any alternative stuffing, they contented themselves with piling, one on top of another, four or five layers of half-empty pasta shells with barely a bit of wild grass to add flavor.

The "complementary" or accompanying dishes define themselves in relation to the main subjects in the syntactical structure of the meal. Antipasti, intermezzi, accompanying dishes, or desserts (as we usually call them today) may precede, accompany, or follow. One could perhaps see in sauces a role analogous to that of grammatical morphemes, emptied of autonomous meaning but essential (like conjunctions and prepositions) in determining the nature and quality of the main characters.

The role of condiments is more like that of the adjectival or adverbial function of the grammar. The choice of condiments can actually be tied not only to economic reasons (the availability of resources), but also to rituals (in Christian Europe, the liturgical calendar and its obligations to eat lean or fat), which endow foods with the spatial-temporal classification typical of adverbs. The option of lard versus oil, with the possible local variation of butter, signifies belonging to a region, to a society, to a culture, but also communicates the day, the week, and the time of year.

In conclusion, food acquires full expressive capacity thanks to the rhetoric that in every language is its necessary complement. Rhetoric is the adaptation of speech to the argument, to the effects one wants to arouse or create. If the discourse is food, that means the way in which it is prepared, served, and eaten.

Adelchi (son of the vanquished king of the Lombards) slipped into the banquet hall of Charlemagne in order to convey to the emperor his own presence and his vengeful defiance. By coming to eat "like a starving lion devouring his prey," Adelchi meant to ascribe to voracity the task of expressing strength, courage, and that sense of animal vigor that the aristocratic society of the high Middle Ages perceived as the founding principle of its own identity.

The silent mealtime ritual of the monks, accompanied by the reading of the sacred texts they had to listen to during meals without saying a word, goes in an entirely different direction. That ritual is expressed both in the monks' way of eating and in the foods consumed, with a self-control and a self-discipline that their rules and life choices imposed. Other rhetorical forms, taken as examples from the society of our own time, are those that signify the speed (often only imaginary) of a working lunch, in contrast with the long, leisurely ceremonial of a wedding banquet or the family dinner celebrating Christmas.

# Substitutions and Annexations

The strong structural and organizational quality of food systems is reflected in their propensity for replicating reference models. If within a system each element occupies a precise place, the first objective will be to maintain and preserve it. Within the Mediterranean and European food tradition, a particularly interesting example to pursue is that of bread.

History teaches that in cases of unforeseen food shortages or famine, when the usual range of food products is unexpectedly diminished, complex survival strategies are put to work. Though these may vary widely, they nonetheless are bound together by this general rule: while in a forced estrangement from usual practices, the strategies continue to adhere as closely as possible to the basic individual culture and to the familiar, already known "language."

The prevalent attitudinal posture is that of *substitution*: identify something that can be used in place of something else.

Chronicles report inventions of all kinds to adapt available resources to known techniques and practices. Bread, if wheat was in short supply, was made with inferior grains. (Of course, for the underclasses, this was accepted practice even in normal times.) Or else one might have recourse to vegetables (above all, fava beans), or, in mountainous regions, to chestnuts (the mountaineers called it "tree bread"). Then, in even harder times, one downgraded further to acorns, then to roots and to wild grasses.

"During this year," wrote Gregory of Tours, referring to events at the end of the  sixth century, "a great famine oppressed the Gauls. Many made their bread with grape seeds or with hazelnut blossoms, others with the roots of crushed ferns, dried and reduced to powder, mixed with a bit of flour. Others made their bread with grass cut in the fields." In extreme cases of penury they even used dirt. In the year 843, according to the *Annals* of Saint Bertin, "In many places men were forced to eat dirt mixed with a bit of flour and baked into a bread shape." The ancient image of a nurturing earth here has left the realm of metaphor to become a literal reality (in fact, within certain categories of humus, there are in fact some soils that are actually edible). But note the expression used by the chronicler: the earth was "baked," then shaped to look like bread (*in panis speciem*). The appearance, the shape, the morphology of the food is what guarantees continuity of the particular food system.

The "bread of famine" recurs often in reference sources. In 1032–33, Raoul Glaber recounts, "An experiment there took place that did not succeed but was tried anyway. They extracted a white sand, somewhat like clay, and mixing it with available amounts of flour and bran, obtained from it loaves, and in so doing sought to escape hunger." Unfortunately, they did so with no positive result, and moreover with serious negative hygienic consequences.

On the other hand, as was rightly noted by Pierre Bonnassier, this was a more "rational" response to famine, before the descent into other forms of behavior induced by panic or by madness. Only the giving up of long consecrated conventions in the methods of preparing and cooking food, not the consumption of certain substances, can be viewed as a sign of the abdication of one's human identity, and of a descent into animality. To eat grasses "like animals," neither processing them nor cooking them—that is the decisive step.

Referring to the dramatic famine in southern Italy in the year 1058, another chronicler of the time, Godfrey Malaterra, informs us that the poor took acorns from pigs, grinding them with other improvised ingredients. The famished poor then tried to bake the acorns into bread. This act of desperation remains a cultural act, which uses survival techniques developed and transmitted orally by generations of starving people, "as is the habit of the poor" (*sicut pauperibus mos est*). "They mix grass and a bit of flour," observed a chronicler recording the famine that took place in Swabia in 1099.

Scientific texts didn't fail to take up the matter. In the Middle Ages numerous references to "famine breads" are found in agronomy treatises in Muslim Spain. "These mobilize in the service of everyday food a complex know-how" (Lucie Bolens), derived from the agronomic, pharmacological, and dietetic tradition of the ancients.

To start out from grains, legumes, and foraged plants; go all the way to domesticated vegetables and fruits; and then arrive at herbs and wild roots, nuts, and medicinal plants implies a sequence of techniques that progressively distance themselves from the norm and require greater attention and care. Ibn al-Awwan teaches how to use fruit that would not naturally be edible but became so, thanks to treatments born from observation and, mark it well, from *tasting*. "One needs to test the basic flavor of these plants and to try to eliminate it using the suitable procedures. When the taste has dissipated, dry the fruit, grind it, then proceed to the *bread-making.*"

In this context what seems to me to be particularly noteworthy is the ongoing presence of continuous and direct references to so-called normal food practices. If we turn back to the imagery of food as a linguistic system, it would be like introducing variations into the lexicon, not (within the limits of the possible) into the morphological and syntactical structure of discourse. Even this can be modified, of course, but only in the wake of important, profound, even traumatic changes. We have already seen such a case, when, for example, we considered the food crisis that in the seventeenth century had struck Naples. The model of traditional food consumption based on meat and greens with accompanying grains was transformed into a new model, which assigned pasta (along with cheese as a condiment) the brand-new role of solitary "main course." On the other hand, this change was an expression, with numerous variants, of the basic tendency of European food in the final centuries of the Middle Ages, and subsequent centuries of the early modern era. The lower layers of society, especially the rural but also the urban, moved toward ever more narrowly focused grain-based consumption, whereas meat, thanks to the mechanisms of economic and social stratification brought about by the interaction of property, production, and marketplace, was defined ever more as an elite product (remaining so at least until the nineteenth and early twentieth centuries).

The mechanism of substitution at times takes on different dimensions, forsaking the realm of contingency by solidly incorporating the variant within the system. Phenomena of this kind appear above all in the presence of new products. In the first centuries of the Christian era the meal based on rye and oats (initially known as wild plants) coincided in Europe with a dramatic decline in wheat. But the most notable and dramatic example is that of American products, which invaded Europe (after the conquest and subjugation of the two new continents) between the end of the fifteenth and the middle of the sixteenth centuries.

The attitude toward these new arrivals, as normally happens in such cases, was one of great curiosity but also of great caution, so much so that it took more or less three centuries for these products to be adopted definitively. Their absorption into the European diet (as well as that of other regions around the world) was so profound and "systematic" that it would be difficult today to imagine Europe without corn or potatoes, tomatoes or peppers—or without hot pepper, which in certain of our own traditions (one thinks of the cooking of Calabria, or elsewhere in Europe, of Hungarian cuisine) has become so indigenous as to make one forget its exotic origins. But such an eventful juxtaposition is instructive, because it shows the capacity of food systems to evolve and change, while at the same time reaffirming their own identity, regenerating themselves thanks to external add-ons, while assimilating the unknown. These are familiar processes on both psychological and cultural levels. In the case in point, the "hook" consists of treating—or, as we shall soon see, *believing* one can treat—new products by traditional procedures and methods of food preparation.

Of course, the spread of new products was encouraged above all by need. Faced with the enormous productivity of American plants, collective hunger had overcome any reservation or fear. In addition, the mechanisms of adaptation were decisive. When, in the eighteenth century, the potato began to work its way into the fields and onto the tables of the European peasantry, agronomists and intellectuals, Augustine Parmentier, foremost among them, issued propaganda for the tuber, seeking to convince the farmers (among those not already convinced) that potato flour could be used to make bread (the food that for centuries European peasants had known and desired). The goal itself proved to be illusory but served to make the new product known. The peasants then began to use the potato in other ways, sometimes new, sometimes traditional, among them the use of potatoes in the dough destined for gnocchi, a most popular dish ever since the Middle Ages that for centuries had been made only with flour and bread crumbs. Moreover, nineteenth-century gastronomy did not hesitate to put potatoes to good use in a number of other new and untraditional ways.

Similarly on the cultural level, while the outcome was different, we can cite the evolution of corn. Introduced into the countryside of some European regions as early as the first half of the sixteenth century, the popularity of corn progressively increased over succeeding centuries. Maize had for millennia been the principal food of various American peoples, used by them in many different kinds of cooking, with various condiments, and within diverse gastronomic customs.

However, no one across the Atlantic had ever used corn to make polenta, although this was to become its principal function in Europe. The motive for this "reinterpretation" was simple: In Europe the culinary tradition had been characterized from antiquity by the use of polenta as the central dish of peasant cookery. In ancient Rome it had been made with spelt, in the medieval period with millet and other grains such as "panic" grass and sorghum, besides that very same spelt. The acceptance of the new product was all the more persuasive when it was shown to be adaptable to traditional usage. But this entry of corn into European food habits, taking on the principal grammatical "function" that until then had been served by other products, signified the progressively increasing disappearance of those products from culinary practices and agricultural cultivation.

This process of substitution ultimately affected terminology itself. In certain European dialects and languages, corn, came to "occupy" the very names of older and better-known grains. Corn was called *millet* in France; *melega,* that is, *sorgo* (sorghum) in Italy; in Hungary it was *tengeribúza,* or sea millet; in the Balkans, depending on the locality, corn was called fava, millet, sorghum, wheat, durum wheat. . . .

Different, yet similar, was the European adventure of the tomato. Like corn and the potato, the tomato had trouble establishing itself, and when it did, it was in familiar and recognizable forms. At first it was pan-fried "like mushrooms and eggplant" (so asserts the sixteenth-century botanist and gastronome Costanzo Felici). But the decisive event marking the tomato's consecration was its transformation into an accompanying sauce. Tomato sauces had been used as early as the seventeenth century to accompany meat and fish (first in Spain, then in Italy). In nineteenth-century Italy tomato sauce was launched on its now official mission of adding taste and color to pasta. And that assignment was an enduring triumph!

In this way the tomato was adapted to a configuration or physiognomy typical of the European tradition: From the Middle Ages on, culinary treatises had devoted ample space to the preparation of sauces, as the indispensable accompaniment to all dishes, above all, but not exclusively, those of fish and meat. And so the tomato was received into the cuisines of the old continent only after its morphological reduction into something familiar, in this case a sauce, which made it fully compatible with traditional usages, while at the same time introducing a new note of taste and color.

Every *new entry* (sic) of a food was like the appearance of a new vocabulary of a language. Morphemes and new words in some way took the place of the old terms, provoking their disappearance or relegating them to marginality.

If corn destroyed the medieval tradition of millet and sorghum, the success of the potato accelerated a rapid decline in the importance of turnips, which had been absolutely central in models of peasant food consumption. In the same way, this time on the tables of the rich, the North American turkey replaced the peacock, taking over the latter's extravagant theatrical functions, so dear to medieval aristocrats. The chili pepper, in contrast, became the "poor people's spice," thereby helping to plug a lack of supply by a surge in "plebeian" demand (as suggested by Dominique Fournier), modeled on upper-class consumption.

Similar developments can be documented with beverages. The spread of tea and coffee, from the seventeenth century on, signaled a drop of demand and supply in the consumption of wine and beer. The new products succeeded in fact in taking on, thanks to the self-serving complicity of commercial companies, some of the traditional roles played by alcoholic beverages. Ever since antiquity, these had been in use for a very wide swath of occasions justifying their consumption (nutritional, convivial, celebratory, ritual . . . ), thereby defining themselves as all-purpose consumer goods, practically without competition.

The new products, to differing extents and according to different locales and social groupings, broke up this monopoly and went on to take over a share of its functions. Tea took over from wine and beer as the socializing drink during daytime, but in some cases, also as the beverage accompanying food during meals. In addition, English and Dutch physicians (curiously, of those very countries commercially invested in promotional campaigns favoring the new drinks!) did not hesitate to propose tea as a panacea for a wide range of ailments, just as medieval doctors had done with wine or as certain French doctors in the seventeenth century did with coffee.

The intersection of economic, political, and fiscal interests whirling around these new products is too strong for us not to consider as suspect the self-interest of medical science (phenomena limited only to the *ancien régime*). But what I want to underline here is once again the *structural* dimension of food consumption and habits—open to innovation and novelty only at the cost of changes based on substitutional more than incremental mechanisms, or else on a transfer of functions from one product to another. This clearly has happened if we consider the historical evolution of European food consumption. If we then contrast Western society with Eastern (Chinese, Indian, Japanese, etc.), we find that the latter traditionally did not have the habitual use of beer and wine. There, in Asia, it is often tea that fulfills the same role played by beer and wine in Europe. Obversely, the appearance of wine or beer on Asian tables (linked in the twentieth century to fashions from abroad or to the prosperity of new productive realities) works against the traditional consumption of tea. This is exactly the opposite of what took place in Europe between the eighteenth and nineteenth centuries.

# Tell Me How Much You Eat
# and I'll Tell You Who You Are

Jacques Le Goff has written that in the Middle Ages food was the "first opportunity for the ruling strata of society to show off their superiority." Through luxury and gastronomic ostentation they expressed what he termed "class-oriented behavior."

There was an obvious justification for this behavior: the availability of food resources was then everyone's primary preoccupation (one could say *obsession*). In this context, an abundance of food indicated a situation of social privilege and power.

Incidentally, this was not a reality exclusive to the Middle Ages. All traditional societies and cultures are marked by hunger, or to state it better, by the *fear* of hunger. That fear could indeed become true hunger after years of famine, epidemics, and war—the three scourges against which one implores divine protection. More often it remained simply a fear, understood both as the psychological attitude of individuals and also, above all, as a culturally shared reality, a collective preoccupation reflected in actions, choices, and behavior.

This *necessity* for food to function as a guarantor of daily survival is a very simple idea that in the current society of abundance risks being shunted into the background. Need for food expresses itself as well and first of all in a *desire for quantity*, the desire, that is, for a full belly and the well-lined purse that provides for it. Quality matters greatly, of course, but comes *afterward*.

The ruler therefore defined himself initially as a big eater. According to the report of Liutprando da Cremona in 888, Duke Guido di Spoleto was rejected as king of the Franks because it came to be known that he ate too little. "He cannot rule us if he is satisfied with a modest meal," his electors asserted at the time. This verdict amounted to stating that the very fact of eating a lot, and managing to consume more food than others, was not just a simple consequence of one's privileged situation (a *can do*), but rather tended to represent a kind of social obligation (a *should do*). That imperative thus became a norm for "class behavior" in which the lord could not come in as lacking heft, at the risk of questioning the established order.

Voracious appetite was also linked to a physical and muscular concept of power, which above all saw in the chief a warrior-like bravery. As the strongest, most vigorous of all, and the most able, he must ingest enormous quantities of food. This became the sign (and at the same time the means of assertion) of a typically animal-like, even bestial superiority over his fellow men.

In fact, the onomastic associations of the warrior were often borrowed from the animal kingdom: In the ranks of medieval nobility one could scarcely count the numbers of "Wolves," "Bears," "Lions," and "Leopards." Note that these are all carnivorous animals, since it is above all to meat that the noble warrior owes his force and courage. According to a cultural image (but at the same time a "scientific" one), meat is endowed with the power to nourish the body, to harden its muscles, and to confer upon the warrior both strength and the legitimacy of his power to lead.

Cultural images these, because to eat means to kill animals, and, for the noble classes especially, wild game slain at the end of exhausting hunts and in veritable duels simulate war in strategy and the use of arms. The hunt trains one for military activity and at the same time provides the very foods that give one the strength to fight. The circle is closed and perfect, both on a technical and on a symbolic level. Dietetic science in turn confirms this, identifying in meat the manly food par excellence, the perfect food for increasing robustness and body strength.

We find this assessment in medical treatises from the medieval period, which differ, in this matter at least, from the Greco-Roman tradition. The latter was a farming culture, which did not hesitate to place bread at the center of its food system and to designate bread as the ideal food for man, for the city-dweller as well as for the soldier. This *ancient* image was later elevated into the myth of the Farmer General, namely Cincinnatus. Now the relevant medieval myth became that of the Sovereign-Hunter.

With the passing of centuries the recurring theme of food quantity as a function of power and social prestige gradually decreased. Power itself was conceived of in a different way, no longer as a manifestation of physical force, to be reaffirmed each time and reconquered on the field of combat, but rather as an acquired right, a legitimate exercise of a function lying within an ordained hereditary path.

This transition from a *nobility through deed* to a *nobility of entitlement*, expressions coined by Marc Bloch to indicate two differing social models characterizing the high and low Middle Ages, respectively, found an immediate counterpart in systemic food models. To eat in quantity was at first a capacity, then became, as we have said, the demonstration of a physical superiority over one's fellow men. With time this was transformed into a right or privilege that one *could* (but not necessarily *should*) exercise. From then on, what did matter was no longer consuming more food than one's fellow diners, but having at one's disposal more food on the table (so as to distribute it to companions, guests, servants, and dogs).

In this fashion the "language of food" developed a content ever more markedly ostentatious, stagy, and theatrical. Between the fourteenth and fifteenth centuries, and even in succeeding centuries, lasting until the threshold of the contemporary, showy display became the distinctive characteristic of aristocratic food privilege, one rigidly formulated by court ceremonials in a precise, even arithmetical way.

Peter III of Aragon wanted differences in rank to be marked at the table with numerical precision, "since at meals it is only just and fair that some be honored more than others, depending on their rank in the social hierarchy." Thus reads the *Ordinacions* of 1344. "We want our own platters to be filled with the food needed for eight diners"; food for six will be placed in the dishes of the royal princes, archbishops, and bishops; food for four in the dishes of the other prelates and knights seated at the king's table. Rules inspired by the same logic were still valid in the nineteenth century, at the Neapolitan court of the Bourbons.

Formalization of quantities, moreover, did not exclude heavy eating as an attribute of the ruling classes. Gout, which spread among the aristocracy of the seventeenth to eighteenth centuries, is a kind of professional disease, linked to the modalities of food consumption (too much food, too much meat) that depended more on social conformity than on personal taste. From this resulted, as an esthetic ideal, a general appreciation of a robust body. To be fat, a sign of wealth and well-being, is to be beautiful. As the heroine of a Goldoni comedy proclaims: "If you want to be mine, I want you beautiful, fat and hearty." But even in our own time, who has not heard a grandmother say, "What a beautiful, chubby baby!" In this way one can explain linguistic usage that, weighed against today's culture, would have sounded paradoxical. The prosperous Florentine bourgeoisie, which celebrated its own economic and political triumph, labeled itself *popolo grasso*—fat populace. A rich city, Bologna, for centuries entrusted the promotion of its own image to its "fatness."

Indices of different attitudes are not lacking. Thinness and svelteness can be positive attributes. So we read of slimming diets undertaken not for reasons of health (about which the physician Galienus had already spoken in Roman times in a treatise devoted to the subject), but instead for aesthetic reasons. In premodern cultures, however, these are marginal and culturally condemned phenomena (unless the fasting be to attain sainthood, as was practiced by the ascetics of the desert and forest). The rounded shapes of the nudes in Greek, Roman, renaissance, and baroque paintings and sculptures suggest, even proclaim, the most appreciated aesthetic ideal. It is surely not obesity that is the goal to be pursued; nonetheless, the thin body does not arouse desire. "One must beware of thin people," Shakespeare writes somewhere.

The positive values of thinness, linked to those of speed, productivity, and efficiency seem to have been put forth as a new cultural and aesthetic model in the works of eighteenth-century bourgeois intellectuals who opposed the old order in the name of new ideologies and political hypotheses.

For example, a hugely provocative social tsunami was generated by a new food product, coffee. Touted as the beverage of bourgeois intelligence and efficiency, coffee was expected to undo the laziness and obtuseness of the traditional aristocracy. Running parallel with that idea was the opposition of the thin to the fat, and it is certainly not coincidental that this subversive drink was categorized by doctors as "dry" (with reference to Galienus's classification), and therefore "dehydrating." As a replacement for wine and beer ("warm" drinks and rich, we would say, in calories), use of coffee also implied an overturning of the most widely held aesthetic canons.

Nineteenth-century Puritanism, harking back to certain aspects of penitential medieval Christianity, also contributed to the reaffirmation of this image of a thin, lithe, productive, and bourgeois body that sacrifices itself, or its heft, to produce wealth and worldly goods.

Little by little, as early as in the nineteenth century, and then especially in the twentieth, consuming large amounts of food and being fat ceased being a privilege or a representation of social superiority. Faced with the increasing democratization of consumer goods brought about by the inexorable logic of industrial food production, new social classes were allowed access to the groaning board. And since, as Fernand Braudel has taught us, pleasures too widely shared quickly lose their attractiveness, it is hardly surprising that the revolution in consumer goods suggested new models of behavior to the elite classes. The custom of eating heartily and ostentatiously, meanwhile, traditionally ascribed to the upper classes, became redefined downward to become a "popular" practice of the middle and lower bourgeoisie, and ultimately also of the urban proletariat and rural peasantry.

In the middle nineteenth century the Milanese author Giovanni Rajberti, published a manual of good manners, the first in Italy destined not for the nobility but for the middle classes: *The Art of Hospitality Explained to the People*. It was important to address these instructions to the people, the author insisted, since the aristocrats already knew how to behave, thanks to long-standing familiarity with banquets. The people, on the other hand, needed to be instructed, especially in matters of moderation and balance. At the table of the popular classes, in point of fact, "there reigned a real fear of never paying sufficient tribute to one's host and his food. The result was that these lower classes moved into a kind of virtual food orgasm, making them go way beyond the deliberation, restraint and know-how that are those first necessary components of the beautiful in all the arts. The result: overly generous heaped dishes, too heavily seasoned and flavored, and a preponderance of foods characteristically and oppressively spicy and stimulating."

Above all, there remained the popularity (shared for a time with the elite classes) of epic narrations of the great eaters and insatiable gluttons. The newly powerful meanwhile had developed other forms of distinctiveness: to eat little, and to eat mostly vegetables. The food model and the aesthetic of thinness, enriched with hygienic health implications, spread considerably in Europe in the first half of the twentieth century.

After the devastating experience of the world war had brought back hunger, however, traditional food models temporarily regained the upper hand. In the 1950s, the female figures on advertising posters were characterized preferably by images of a generously endowed bodily shape glowing with health. It was only beginning in the 1970s and 1980s that the cult of thinness truly triumphed. What happened was that on the cultural plane there was a reversal of the food dynamic: the danger and fear of excess had replaced the danger and fear of hunger.

The abundance of food typical of the postmodern industrial age poses new problems, whose possible solutions remain difficult for a culture historically marked by the fear of hunger and by a desire to consume food in quantity. Attitudes and behaviors have remained conditioned by this. The irresistible attraction of excess, which a thousand years' history of hunger had imprinted on bodies and minds, now began to take its toll. In prosperous countries, diseases caused by food excesses, formerly the privilege of the few, became the afflictions of the many, a mass phenomenon of illness due to unhealthy overeating replacing the traditional diseases formerly due to malnutrition and famine.

This phenomenon paved the way for a hitherto unknown form of fear (*fear of obesity*, as Americans have baptized it). It overturned the atavistic fear of hunger, and like the latter, acted most particularly on individual psyches regardless of objective circumstances.

Investigations have shown that more than half the people who, thinking themselves overweight, dealt with the problem by giving up various foods were not in fact so. The core of the problem seems to be the gap between economic development and cultural processing.

We have moved into an age of abundance with the mental equipment constructed for a world of hunger. An icon of this contradiction would be the archipelago of Tonga in the Pacific, the country with the highest rate of obesity in the world, and whose King Tuafa'ahau Tupuo IV entered the Guinness Book of Records as the "fattest ruler in the world." Here we have the expression and model of a traditional society overwhelmed by an abundance of food after thousands of years of difficulty and yearning. *Noblesse oblige:* Tupuo IV must have yielded to the need to face up to his own growing health problems as well as to those of his subjects. So he forced himself onto a strict diet that in several months brought him from 200 to 130 kilos. Moreover, in a country where being fat had always been a sign of nobility and social prestige, Tupuo IV launched, and had his government sponsor, a slimming competition. This royal saga could be the symbol of a balance needing to be restored, of a *cultural* challenge aimed at rebuilding and reshaping attitudes on food issues, possibly with reciprocal cordiality.

# The How, the Why, and the Wherewithal

"Tell me what you eat and I'll tell you who you are." When Anthelme Brillat-Savarin wrote these words (*Physiology of Taste*, 1825), his perspective was above all psychological and behavioral: ways of eating revealed the personality and character of an individual. Placed within a historical perspective, however, the aphorism takes on a broader significance, one that is social or collective rather than individual. Traditional cultures understand the quality of food to be the direct expression of a particular level of hierarchical membership in society. It is an expression that extends in both directions: The manner of feeding oneself *derives from* a determinate social membership, while at the same time *revealing* or *expressing* that membership.

So the quality of the food, in addition to the quantity, has a strong communicative power and immediately expresses social identity, as was apparent in the traditional European food culture developed during the Middle Ages. Documents show clearly that the noble classes defined themselves above all as consumers of meats (and, as we have seen, of game, in particular). Meat, we recall, is the food most directly associated with the idea of both symbolic and functional power. The image of the peasant, in contrast, is linked to the fruits of the land: grains, vegetables, broths, and soups are his "natural" food, at least according to the images provided by literature. In fact, we know that the peasant of the high Middle Ages also consumed reasonable quantities of meat. Prowling the woods was part of his daily activity, and hunting and animal husbandry provided much of his food intake.

With the passage of centuries, the demographic increase and the spread of cultivated land area, along with the attendant loss of grazing land and forests, produced a broader social phenomenon: the exclusion of the rural classes from entitlements authorizing access to and exploitation of these resources. These rights became the increasingly exclusive prerogative of the nobility (as were were wild game and most other meats), with the possible exception of pork, which remained, in fact and in the collective perception, a meat for the peasantry.

Other things changed as well with the passage of time. Near the close of the Middle Ages, the image of the nobility and the practice and exercise of power were no longer the same as in earlier centuries. The nobleman was no longer *only* the warrior, and physical strength (as we have said) was no longer his most important attribute.

"Courtliness" (derived from "courtesy") was born—a new way of living and behaving in society. The sign of nobility henceforth was no longer the capacity to eat in quantity, but rather (and above all) the ability to know how to distinguish the good from the bad, and ultimately to master self-restraint and self-control—virtues unthinkable in earlier times as models for aristocrats. In chivalric or courtly romances, the young nobleman was subjected to this test: to reject food not worthy of his social rank, and to understand at a glance what food would be appropriate for him.

Other forms of social identity mediated by food were those that concerned the clergy: the monks and the priests. Their statutes implied a precise code regulating food behavior. Monks, in particular, found that code writ in stone, with rules overseeing and governing every act of their daily life. A fundamental rule was the partial or total

exclusion of meat from the diet, though there were, of course, exceptions governing all or only some animals (often only quadrupeds).

In any case the monastic (like the aristocratic) concern with food
revolved principally around meat. The example is not an obvious
one. If the motivations for the exclusion of meats are multiple and
complex, they are doubtless the expression of a will to reject a lifestyle of carnivorous eating culturally long synonymous with the exercise of power, force, and violence. Denying oneself meat means distancing oneself from the enticement of power. It was not coincidental
that the majority of monks issued from noble lineage. In their "con-
version" a reversal of eating habits played a prominent role. The symbolic importance of renouncing meat is reflected in the monks' preference for "poor people's food," borrowed from the peasant world as
a sign of spiritual humility: greens, vegetables, grains. To be sure, we
are dealing here with a willing renunciation, not one made under
duress and dictated by poverty. It is in this act of free will that there
lies the redemptive value of the experience.

On the dietetic plane, one that is scientific and no longer symbolic, the correspondences are perfect. Meat, which nourishes the
flesh and strengthens the body, is unsuitable for those who have, to
the detriment of base bodily exigencies, made a commitment to the
spiritual life. For these a "light diet" is suitable, one that removes as
far as possible from perception the gastric awareness of corporeality,
while favoring a transcendentally decorporealized ascent toward
heaven. Thus the monastic rules, while generally excluding meat, often make an exception for winged creatures. What flies is therefore
lighter and "higher," and better suited to a spiritual diet.

The fact remains that, beginning with the final centuries of the
Middle Ages, the foods most appreciated by Italian and European
aristocrats were no longer large animals like stag, wild boar, or bear,

but poultry such as pheasant and partridge. This change in taste provides an insight into the cultural changes that had taken place in the interim. Centuries earlier these would have been considered monks' foods. If at a certain juncture they became the preferred foods on the lordly table, that is because the nobility too had changed. The lords had become less warrior-like and more political, less committed to the exercise of physical force and more to the administrative and political management of power. In some cases they were even intellectuals who surrounded themselves with artists, musicians, and men of letters!

In the sixteenth century, Dr. Castore Durante da Gualdo proclaimed, in what was almost a secular version of the monastic suggestion, that birds are the ideal food for those who dedicate themselves to works of wit and intellect.

The links between food consumption and lifestyles defined in relation to social hierarchies developed in various ways in centuries closer to our own. The motif of *quality* became clearer. Consumers now took for granted that the domain of social privilege expressed itself in the right—or duty—to procure food products of ever higher quality. However, there were still correspondences between typologies of foods and beverages and the typologies of the consumers themselves. For example, in eighteenth-century Europe, coffee was considered the preeminent bourgeois drink, whereas chocolate was aristocratic. What was defined here was a clearly ideological antithesis: the former awoke and stimulated the mind to work and to be productive; whereas the latter was a drink for the torpid and lazy. In the following century, however, coffee had already become a popular beverage in France, as had tea in Holland and England.

Symbols are a cultural product and change from one era to another, as from one society to another, just as the acceptable social behavior of society and individuals changes. The social significance of the potato changed in the opposite direction from the beverages. Europeans of the eighteenth century had no doubt about potatoes being peasant food (if not fodder); while in the following century the tuber was accorded right of entry into the *haute cuisine* of the bourgeoisie and aristocracy.

Similar phenomena take place under our very own eyes. The inversion of meaning is linked to the transition from a society of hunger to one of abundance. This transition leads us, for example, to upgrade into emblematic signs of up-market social standing certain products traditionally viewed as poor and rustic (the lower categories of grains—millet, rye, barley, and spelt, long tied to images of rural hunger—come to mind). These were in contrast with grains formerly intended for the rich, but that today are snubbed in turn by elite diets. The anthropologist Tullio Seppilli called this phenomenon a form of folkloristic revival. Or it may just be one of the ways by which contemporary society recovers a past that had distorted the values of its signifiers. Fraught with ambiguity, and mystifying, in the context of a simple recovery of olden times, this process is a fully legitimate one if practiced with full awareness that what is at stake is building a *new* culture.

# Food and the Calendar: A Lost Dimension?

A traditionally strong aspect of culinary culture, one largely lost to us today, is the calendar of feasting and fasting days. Man and God endowed food with values meaningfully linked to the flow of time. Traditional societies directly and programmatically associated the preparation and consumption of this or that food with a recurring date in the calendar. Christmas had its foods, as did Easter; Mardi Gras was not Lent, and the summer was not winter.

But *nota bene*: even in this "calendrification" of food the *cultural* aspects took precedence over the *natural*. To be sure, the cyclical rhythm of the seasons found an immediate and direct response in the types of food to be served. Physicians from Hippocrates on recommended observing this correspondence: eat "cold" in the hot months and eat "hot" in the cold months. All possible variations of this game were linked to the theory of the four humors.

Nevertheless, it is important to reemphasize what we have already observed. This fine-tuning between man and nature did *not* always play out to a positive conclusion. The cycle of seasons could hold surprises, and the primary gastronomic goal was always to modify foods in order to be able to save them as preserved beyond their seasonality. In contrast, the elite classes, in fact, took pride in consuming fresh fruits and greens out-of-season, importing them (*fresh!*) from faraway places.

Other cycles, *artificial* in various ways, decisively determined the food calendar and its nutritive rhythms. The church calendar, from the fourth century on, obliged all Christians to observe the distinction between "fat" and "lean" days; that is, to eat or not to eat animal products and fats, substituting, according to the liturgical year, oil for lard, fish for flesh, greens for cheese. The church calendar always reinforced traditional customs by pointing out, often with the enticement of certain sweet foods, the continuity of the principal holiday traditions—for example, the Hebrew Passover and Christian Easter.

In medieval Italy every holiday had its own food. Orvieto's Simone Prudenzani, a writer endowed with a good sense of humor, could smile at the excessive piety of certain ladies who, at each recurrent holiday, never missed a celebratory food:

> Se voi sapeste la divotione
> Ch'ell'à nelle lasagnie di Natale,
> En le farrate ancor de Carnovale,
> Nel cascio et huova della Sensione,
> Nell'ocha d'Onnisanti et maccheroni
> Del Giobia grasso et anco nel maiale
> De Santo Antonio et ne l'agnel pasquale,
> Nol porrìa dire in sì piccol sermone.
> Per tucto l'oro ch'è sotto a le stelle,
> Non lasciarebbe 'l dì de la Cenciale
> Che non mangiasse un quarto de frittelle;
> Vin dolce et grande ancor molto ce vale
> Et non ce mettrìa acqua per covelle
> Perché dice che giova ad omne male.

[If you only knew her devotion to lasagna on Christmas Day, to spelt during Carnival, and cheese and eggs on Ascension Day, and to goose or duck on All Saints' Day, and macaroni on Fat Thursday, and pork on Saint Anthony's, and Easter lamb. No one could begin to describe her pi-

*ety and devotion in so short a priestly sermon, I could not do it if you paid me all the gold under the stars. No feast day would she let go by without a share of pancakes and sweet wine or the equivalent; nor would she water down her wine. Because she says all these cure all ailments!]*

It is certainly possible (as a matter of fact probable) that some of these products and dishes had imposed themselves on holidays also because they were tied to the "natural" calendar. Lamb at Easter is ordained in the Biblical narrative (as are the bitter herbs and unleavened bread for the Hebrews), but one cannot deny that this is a particularly "appropriate" moment to taste it. So to eat pork for the feast of Saint Anthony in January is "economically correct," because it is at that time of the year that the pig is butchered. The statement holds equally true for local specialties linked to specific holidays on the religious or state calendars. On the other hand, the same is not always true, and above all, does *not* apply to many other foods, among them pastas (lasagna, macaroni, etc.) and many flour-based sweets (frittelle, panettoni, etc.), spread throughout the year by the multiplicity of holidays. These are not limited to specialized seasonal production.

Above all, calendrically speaking, there are the variously shaped breads with their toppings or fillings that mark seasonal differences. But even here various ingredients like raisins or candied fruit, cinnamon, and other sweet spices (typical enhancements of holiday sweets) do not of themselves suggest a direct link to a particular season. Rather, their use at this time is that of a product "put down" to be preserved long-term. *Panettone* suggests Christmas to us not so much because it is produced in an appropriately "christmasy" way, but because it is traditionally made at that time. That is why it is hard to sell panettone even today outside of the Christmas season. The age-old significance of the food calendar may no longer be the same, but it is hard to make it vanish altogether.

# Identity, Exchange, Traditions, and "Origins"

The analogy between food and language that we have made by juxtaposing the two as semiological systems, beyond (in the case of food) their material reality, characterizes both as codes of communication. They convey symbolic and *signifying* meanings of widely differing kinds (economic, social, political, religious, ethnic, aesthetic), both inside and outside the societies that express them.

Like spoken language, the food system contains and conveys the culture of its practitioner; it is the repository of traditions and of collective identity. It is therefore an extraordinary vehicle of self-representation and of cultural exchange—a means of establishing identity, to be sure, but also the first way of entering into contact with a different culture. Eating the food of the "other" is easier, it would seem, than decoding the other's language. Far more than spoken language itself, food can serve as a mediator between different cultures, opening methods of cooking to all manner of invention, cross-pollination, and contamination.

The two notions of identity and exchange, often called up when dealing with food culture, are contrasted at times as though the exchange, that is, the confrontation of different identities, were itself the obstacle to the preservation of those identities, and of the cultural heritage that each society recognizes in its own past.

This kind of perspective, which readily inspires reticence when faced with "difference," arouses fear of contamination and more or less aggravated forms of narrow-mindedness and intolerance. History is generally summoned as the source of more or less mythical "origins" or "roots" that one retraces to preserve one's own identity. But history shows us exactly the opposite: cultural identities are *not* metaphysical realities ("the spirit of the people") and are not even inscribed in the genetic inheritance of a society. These identities change and are redefined incessantly, adapting themselves to always-new situations determined by contact with different cultures.

An exemplary case is that of the European Middle Ages, which, as we have already shown, witnessed the formation of a new culinary and gastronomic identity, substantially innovative with respect to the past. The legacy of that past was nonetheless successfully transmitted, thanks to an extraordinary experiment of contamination, at times even conflict, between cultures both different and to some degree in opposition.

The new civilization, as we know, was born from the grafting of the Roman tradition (taken up and reinforced by Christianity) onto the "barbaric." The culture of bread, wine, and oil intersected with a culture of meat, beer, and animal fats.

What arose from this was a hitherto unknown model of production and consumption in which meat (especially pork for the peasantry) accompanied or joined bread as the basic "core value" of the system. It was a dynamic of mutual integration, one that was simultaneously economic and symbolic, and constituted one of the most interesting episodes in the history of food culture.

In this fashion, bread and pork along with wine actually became the central food symbols of European identity. At that time in history, on the southern shores of the Mediterranean, there arose a new faith, the Islamic, which did not endow bread with equally positive symbolic meaning, while wine and pork were categorically rejected as impure.

Such a turn of events was emblematic of the dynamic character of the history of food, and of the *historic* and therefore changeable nature of all the symbolic identities of food. So, in another historic turn, on the north of the Mediterranean were projected certain values originating elsewhere and that in the past had characterized other cultures. The civilization of bread and wine had been born in the regions of the Afro-Asian Near and Middle East. From the Middle Ages onward, that civilization became primarily European.

However, Islamic cultures did not participate in this change of direction merely in terms of negative otherness. Islam made a crucial contribution to the new gastronomic model soon to take shape in medieval Europe. From the Middle East and from Africa came new plants and new farming techniques: sugarcane, citrus fruits, and greens like eggplant and spinach. Arabs and Saracens introduced the West to the oriental taste for spices—for the bittersweet, the sweet, and the salty. They relaunched models of farming and cooking previously practiced by Roman gastronomy, but now expressed in different and less exclusive forms. They also brought to Europe the planting and culture of rice. In Sicily they introduced the use of dried pasta, a kind of food the Hebrews were also spreading throughout Europe and that was to become enormously popular, especially in Italian regions. So, in this example as well, *tradition* asserted itself and developed very far from its places of *origin*.

*Tradition, Origin:* These are two words we ought to learn to distinguish more precisely. Historians, following the lessons of Marc Bloch, have begun to distrust the "myth of origins" in order to focus more directly on the historical processes of the spread of phenomena.

That these food and cultural identities are the product of history, traceable only partially to environmental and geographical situations, is something we can clearly discover in the process of assembling the so-called Mediterranean diet. This diet was of course superficially made famous (especially by the American media) as the fruit of "ancient wisdom," of a time-tested "tradition."

To speak simply of a "Mediterranean diet" in the singular is a kind of metaphysical abstraction. The singular ignores the extreme variety of situations that geography itself, not to mention history, has created among such regions as, say, Provence and Lebanon, Tunisia and Dalmatia, Sicily and Egypt.

Moreover, many factors constituting this so-called Mediterranean diet are not in fact originally Mediterranean, but rather issue from a fairly recent history of cultural exchanges with the world's other regions and continents.

Today's Mediterranean cuisines have in fact retained little of the ancient diet, except for the use of bread, wine, olive oil, lamb, and onion, but otherwise little else. Of salted and fermented fish sauces like *garum*, once widely used in the ancient era of Greece and Rome and even in the Middle Ages, nothing now remains in the present habits of today's populations. The occasional attempt to resurrect that product, a ritual performed more than anything out of historical curiosity, does not alter the fact that this taste no longer belongs to Mediterranean cuisine. (One does, however, find it in Southeast Asia, particularly in the Vietnamese sauce called *nuoc mâm*.)

Today's Mediterranean flavors actually became prominent only in recent times. As Louis Stouff has shown in his account of Provence—underlining the "modernity" of those traits that today define the personality of Provençal cuisine—eggplant and artichokes were Arabic imports during the late Middle Ages; the flat bean and tomato came from America. Relatively recent as well is the widespread use of olive oil, which was already produced during antiquity, but only in small quantities and largely intended for cosmetic care. Even basil seems not to have been present in the kitchen until the Renaissance.

Vegetables, together a basic component of the so-called Mediterranean diet, had a low profile as a nutritional food during the Middle Ages and beyond. They were a poor expedient for those who could not attain for themselves sufficient meat, still considered the principal constituent factor of any healthy diet.

Besides, many of these vegetables are of Middle Eastern or Asian origin and were diffused among the Mediterranean peoples by the Arabs, but not before the Middle Ages. To these same Arabs, as we have briefly seen, can be traced the origins of rice and the spread of edible pasta (which, some maintain, could have been of Persian origin). Thus, Asia and America have been, like Africa and Europe, essential in determining the characteristics of the food system we usually define as "Mediterranean," and that, besides, is just one of many ways of eating that can be found within this geographical region.

Culinary identities were not inscribed in the heavens.

# Roots: A Metaphor to Use All the Way

The stories we have narrated serve to remind us that every culture, every tradition, every identity is a dynamic, unstable product of history, one born of complex phenomena of exchange, interaction, and contamination. Food models and practices are meeting points among diverse cultures, the fruit of man's travels, of commercial markets, techniques, and tastes from one part of the world to another.

Let us go further: Food cultures (in fact, cultures in general) are so much richer and more interesting when the encounters and exchanges have been lively and frequent. Take, for example, the matter of delineating national boundaries. The quest for roots, when undertaken with a critical methodology, and not screened behind impulsive emotional associations, never succeeds in defining our point of departure (even if distracting us with often outrageous collective imagery).

On the contrary, we find instead a web of increasingly denser threads, ever broader and more complicated, that recede from us, even as we gradually move ever further away from ourselves.

Within this intricate system of relationships and exchanges, it is not the roots but ourselves who are the fixed point: identity does not exist at the outset but rather at the end of the trajectory.

If we really want to speak of roots, let us rely on metaphor all the way, and let us imagine the history of our food culture as a growing—not a shrinking—plant. It gradually burrows into the earth, seeking vital nourishment wherever it can, implanting its roots precisely in places as distant as possible (sometimes unimaginable). The product is on the surface—visible, clear, and well-defined: *that is us.* The roots are underneath—generous, numerous, and diffuse.

It is History that has created us.

# Index

# Index

England, 24, 25, 86; tea in, 112, 126
the Enlightenment, 45–46
environment, 3, 5, 6, 46
etiquette, food, 97, 120
Europe: animal rituals in, 10; class
    in, 23–24; colonialism of, 25–26;
    cuisine of, 31, 50, 62, 86, 134–37;
    fermentation in, 17; mixed food
    culture of, 11–12, 134–37; new
    American foods in, 108–11;
    popular culture in, 36; spread of
    agriculture to, 5, 6

famine, 24, 25, 115, 121; and substi-
    tution, 105–7, 108
fatness: aesthetic of, 118–19; fear of,
    121–22
fats, 64–65. *See also* oils
Felici, Costanzo, 56, 73, 110
fermentation, 16–17
Fertile Crescent, 5
Filoromo, 44
fire, 29–33, 43, 44, 48, 51
fish, 40, 54
Flandrin, Jean-Louis, 62, 72, 84
Florence, 118
fork, 65
four humors, 52–57, 74, 129
Fournier, Dominique, 111
France: coffee in, 126; cuisine of,
    41, 63, 64, 76, 79, 86; regional
    cuisine in, 79, 86, 136; and
    universal cuisine, 76

fruit, 14–15, 53–54, 55, 56, 73–74,
    107

*The Galateo* (Della Casa), 97
Galienus, 51–52, 119
garlic, 38, 54
*garum*, 136
gender, 33, 49–50, 95
Germanic culture, 11–12, 86–87
Germany, 10, 24
*Gilgamesh*, 7
Glaber, Raoul, 106
globalization, 20, 26, 80, 83–89
Goody, Jack, 35
gout, 118
grains, 5, 15, 86, 100, 127; vs. corn,
    110; in mythology, 9–10; and
    substitution, 105–6, 108
Grande Maiale, 10
Greece, ancient, 11, 12, 51, 136
Gregory of Tours, 106
guests, placement of, 95–97
Guido di Spoleto, 116

hamburgers, 88
Harris, Marvin, 71, 72
health, 51–57, 66, 118, 121. *See also*
    dietetics; medicine
herding, 9–12
hermits, 43–45, 94–95, 119
hierarchy, 95–97, 118, 123, 126. *See
    also* class
Hilarion, 44